Tony Evans

DISCOVER YOUR DESTINY

HARVEST HOUSE PUBLISHERS
EUGENE, OREGON

Cover by Rightly Designed, Buckley, Washington

DISCOVER YOUR DESTINY
Copyright © 2013 Tony Evans
Published by Harvest House Publishers
Eugene, Oregon 97402
www.harvesthousepublishers.com

ISBN 978-0-7369-6774-7 (pbk.)
ISBN 978-0-7369-6775-4 (eBook)

The Library of Congress has cataloged the earlier edition as follows:
Evans, Tony, 1949-
Destiny / Tony Evans.
    p. cm.
ISBN 978-0-7369-4997-2 (pbk.)
1. Christian life. I. Title.
BV4501.3.E9155 2013
248.4—dc23
                                            2012029033

Printed in the United States of America
        17 18 19 20 21 22 23 24 25 / BP-KG / 10 9 8 7 6 5 4 3

DISCOVER
YOUR
DESTINY

This book is dedicated to God,

who revealed to me my destiny
and allowed me to help others discover theirs.

CONTENTS

"Your destiny is the customized life calling God has ordained and equipped you to accomplish in order to bring Him the greatest glory and achieve the maximum expansion of His kingdom."

—Dr. Tony Evans

INTRODUCTION

Victor was a Swiss scientist. Having experienced personal tragedy, he sought to address his pain by engrossing himself in an experiment—turning a lifeless object into a living being.

Scouring graveyards and funeral homes, Victor gathered all of the parts and pieces he needed to put together a massive creature that he chose to name after himself: Frankenstein. But the living being he created quickly turned into a monster.

Most of us have seen the movie, but do you know the real tragedy of the story? The monster—after he had been transformed from a lifeless collection of parts into a living being—turned on the very person who created him. In his independence, he turned against his creator, transforming him into a victim.

Christians are not ten feet tall and don't walk around with bolts or dismembered body parts sewn together, but the truth of the film resonates in many lives. Even though we were dead in our trespasses and God gave us life, creating something in us where there was previously nothing, many of God's children have turned on their Creator. Rather than live for Him, they choose to live for themselves—their own wants, desires, emotions, and will. As a result, lives disintegrate, and what had been created for something good quickly devolves into a debacle.

This shows up in the divorce rate as independent people become couples and try to live together. It shows up in the suicide rate as failures lead to depression, hopelessness, and eventually a decision to throw in the towel altogether. It shows up in addictions as people try to numb their pain through chemicals, prescription drugs, overspending, or obsessions. It shows up in corporations or even in ministry as leaders neglect personal or family time and fill their schedules with meetings in order to somehow satisfy an emptiness caused by not living out a divinely ordained destiny.

When you live out your destiny, you don't measure what you have done according to what someone else has done. Nor is your destiny to be confused with a busy life. When your life is filled with purpose, you measure what you have done according to what you were created to do.

> When your life is filled with purpose, you measure what you have done according to what you were created to do.

Many people spend much of their lives trying to be somebody else. Yet this simply reveals that they don't know who they are supposed to be.

Companies often seek to exploit this through a marketing myth that says you can be someone else by buying and wearing a jersey with someone else's number on it, shoes that a celebrity says he or she wears, makeup that actresses say they use, or clothes that models are seen in. Somehow people think that if they can look like, act like, or talk like a star—or perhaps even get close to one—then they will somehow *be* a star. The problem is that they have not yet discovered that they are already stars in their own right. You are a star. You already have your own jersey number. You have your own style. You are special.

Even worse, this seems to be just as prevalent among Christians as it is among non-Christians. Some people say they have a relationship with Jesus Christ and are on their way to heaven, yet they have a hole in them so big you could drive a Mack truck right through it. One of the main reasons people fail to live out their destinies is that they fail to understand why they were created and who created them. They fail to understand this because they fail to understand God's kingdom.

The Bible is not an anthology of random stories. The thread that ties the entire Bible together is the theme of the kingdom. God's goal is to see His rule and authority cover the earth through the expansion of His kingdom. That is God's purpose in history.

Scripture was penned in order to facilitate that one agenda. The unifying central theme of the Bible is the glory of God through the advancement of His kingdom. Every event, story, and personality from Genesis to Revelation is there to stitch that theme together. Without that theme, the Bible becomes a collection of disconnected stories that seem to be unrelated to one another. Similarly, when you don't recognize and incorporate the theme of the kingdom in your own life, your experiences will likewise seem disconnected, unrelated, and random. They will lack the cohesion that your destiny provides. Understanding and embracing God's kingdom is the secret to living with meaning simply because your life is tied to His kingdom. God's kingdom agenda for you and for all others is based on His comprehensive rule over every area of life.

We celebrate our country and our citizenship by reciting the pledge of allegiance and singing the national anthem. But if you have been born again through Jesus Christ, you are part of an even greater kingdom. You are a citizen of the kingdom of God.

Understanding what the kingdom is and how it impacts you is vitally important because it explains your life and purpose. It shows you how things blend together to create an integrated whole. It gives your life meaning. Apart from the kingdom, the events and aspects of your life remain unattached to each other and cannot produce their intended results.

> God's goal is to see His rule and authority cover the earth through the expansion of His kingdom. That is God's purpose in history.

Butter by itself doesn't taste very good. Nutmeg by itself doesn't taste very good. Flour by itself doesn't taste very good. Salt by itself doesn't taste very good. None of these ingredients by themselves would be enough to tempt anyone to taste them. But when a baker measures them and mixes them together for an intended purpose, putting them in the heat of the oven…the smell of the freshly baked cake is enough to lure anyone into the kitchen.

When we believers do not make our lives all about God's kingdom, we segment our lives into various components rather than allowing God to blend them all together toward a greater good. We often quote Romans 8:28: "We know that God causes all things to work together for good to those who love God, to those who are called *according to His purpose.*"

However, the part of the passage that is most often quoted is simply, "All things work together for good." The problem is that all things do not work together for good. To only quote half the verse is to miss the whole meaning. The things that work together for good are those that happen to people who love God and are called according to His purpose. God's purpose is His glory and the advancement of His kingdom as we are conformed to the image of His Son.

When you are living your life according to God's purpose, He will cause all the things in your life to blend together for His good purpose in your life. Otherwise, "all things" that happen to you won't be intentionally connected and used to work toward His good for you.

Today, if you feel as if your life is like butter or flour or nutmeg, begin turning it into something savory by loving God and seeking His destiny for you. When you are committed to Him above all else, He will measure everything in your life—the good, bad, and the bitter—and blend them into something divine. I hope this book will be a practical guide that helps you discover and enjoy the destiny God has planned specifically for you.

PART 1

The Importance of Your Destiny

Concept 1

The great Italian sculptor, painter, architect, and poet Michelangelo once said, "In every block of marble I see a statue as plain as though it stood before me, shaped and perfect in attitude and action. I have only to hew away the rough walls that imprison the lovely apparition to reveal it to the other eyes as mine see it."

In every imperfect, jagged-edged, bulky, unshaped block of marble Michelangelo set his eyes on, he saw the treasure within. He once described the process this way: "I saw the angel in the marble and carved until I set him free." Michelangelo could do this because he didn't see what the marble was; he saw what the marble would be.

He saw a masterpiece.

Friend, you are a masterpiece. In the book of Ephesians, we read this about another Artist: "We are His workmanship, created in Christ Jesus for good works, which God prepared beforehand so that we would walk in them."

The Greek word translated *workmanship* in this verse refers to you, me, and every other child of God. It is *poiēma,* from which we get our English word *poem.* This word denotes a work of art or a masterpiece.[1] You have been made as a work of God—you are His *poiēma.* You weren't created on the assembly line or as a random object thrown together to fill up space or time. When God made you, He went to work—intentionally and delicately crafting your personality, looks, passions, skills…even allowing your imperfections and planting your dreams all into one magnificent work of art. In fact, God did more than plant your dream inside of you. God dreamed a dream for you. Did you know that God has a dream for you? He does.

You are His masterpiece. You are God's dream. What's more, you were made with a purpose. That purpose includes responsible stewardship of God's authority. It includes expanding His dominion. It includes more than merely showcasing your talents. It involves impacting your world for good by ruling the realm where God has positioned you.

Destiny and Authority

When God set about to create Adam and Eve, He said, "Let Us make man in Our image, according to Our likeness; and let them rule" (Genesis 1:26). Theologians often refer to this passage as the initiation of the *dominion covenant*. It reveals that God placed mankind on earth to serve as His stewards over His creation. He placed us here and gave us dominion—the authority to rule. David echoes this covenant in Psalm 8:4-6:

> What is man that You take thought of him
>   And the son of man that You care for him?
> Yet You have made him a little lower than God,
>   And You crown him with glory and majesty!
> *You make him to rule over the works of Your hands;*
>   You have put all things under his feet.

When God gave us dominion, He said it came with two conditions. First, our authority is an extension of His authority. By charging mankind with dominion, God relinquished His direct rule over the things of the earth and now rules through mankind. In essence, He made mankind managers over His creation. Managers don't carry out their own processes, procedures, or initiatives. They oversee tasks and people in a manner that reflects the goals and vision of their superiors.

God is our Superior, and we have been placed on earth to manage His creation under Him.

The second condition of the dominion covenant is that if you rule according to God's intentions, you will receive God's provision. In other words, He will supply all that you need when your decisions are based on His principles and purpose.

However, the reverse of that is true as well. God gives you the freedom to rule your world according to your own goals apart from Him, but if you do, you will lack His provision and His backing, just as any manager would lack the provision of his company should he choose to carry out his own goals and not those of his leadership.

God has designed you to have all that you need to productively rule your world. Yet in spite of this provision, many people today are being ruled by their world rather than ruling the realm in which they have been placed. This can be due to their own personal sin, someone else's sin, or even something as seemingly negligible as setting their own goals above God's. Anytime you operate outside of God's purpose for your life, you will experience the consequences of ruling on your own, such as relational, social, emotional, or financial chaos. Things no longer function as smoothly as they would under God.

> God has designed you to have all that you need to productively rule your world.

I am not saying that if you live according to the will of God, you will never face challenges. There will always be challenges. Even if you do what is right, you will face trials simply because you live in a sin-soaked and fallen environment. In addition, God often uses trials to strengthen and develop you. But Jesus said that if you follow Him, those trials will not overpower you. They will not shake you. In spite of them, you will feel secure and peaceful. "These things I have spoken to you, so that in Me you may have peace. In the world you have tribulation, but take courage; I have overcome the world" (John 16:33).

In other words, the chaos around you shouldn't override the calm within you. Living out your destiny simply means living according to God's divine design within you. It means carrying out the full authority you have been granted and ruling in the realm where He has placed you. It entails fully developing and maximizing the masterpiece known as *you*.

Characteristics of a Masterpiece

You Are Rare

Several characteristics make up a masterpiece. The first one is that a masterpiece is rare. In order for something to be a masterpiece, it cannot have duplicates all over the place. Replicas or prints may exist that reflect the unique nature of the original, but there is only one masterpiece—just as there is only one you. In all of God's family, no one else is like you. You are unique. You are rare, which is exactly how you were designed to be. Knowing that truth should free you from trying to be like someone else, to look like someone else, or to adopt someone else's skills, calling, purpose, or personality. God already has someone else. If you become like someone else, who is going to be you? He made only one you, and *you* are that one.

Maybe as you grew up you were told that you were the wrong gender, the wrong race, or the wrong height. Maybe you felt as if you were born in the wrong place or placed in the wrong family. Perhaps you felt as if you weren't smart enough, skilled enough, fast enough, strong enough, or vocal enough. You may have felt as if you didn't have enough raw potential. But let me tell you something about you. You are a masterpiece—one of a kind. When God created you, He chose every piece about you and planned for you to use it to fulfill your destiny. You are exactly who God intended you to be. And God often uses the weaker and less likely people in this world to accomplish the greatest things. That way He gets the glory, and He knows you will depend on Him to do it. As a masterpiece, you are rare. You are one of a kind.

You Are Special

A masterpiece is special—just like you. In fact, you are so special that God sent His own Son to live for you, die for you, and rise from the dead for you so you can be all that He intended you to be.

You are a masterpiece. Yet until you start believing that you are special, you will not be all that you were created to be. You will not understand that you are qualified to rule. How can you rule your world if you don't think you have the ability to do so? How can you rule your realm if you don't see yourself as a ruler?

Once upon a time, a queen's daughter was slouching in her dining room chair. The queen told her to sit up straight, and she did—only to later slouch back down again. This went on for quite some time until finally, after several rounds of telling her daughter to sit up straight, the queen said, "Sit up, my child. Don't you know who you are?"

Knowing who you are changes your posture. You act differently, think differently, talk differently, walk differently, and live differently—because you *are* different. You are rare; you are special. In fact, you are so special that you are the only you that will ever exist. There will never be another you just like you. You are not an off-the-rack you—you are a custom-made you. You are special.

You Are Valuable

A masterpiece is also valuable. People pay a lot of money to own a masterpiece. In fact, most masterpieces are carefully locked away in secure and protected locations, such as museums and art galleries. Michelangelo's masterpiece *David* stands towering safely in Florence at the Accademia Gallery. The average person could not afford to own it. In fact, the average person cannot even afford to travel to Italy just to view it. That speaks volumes to the value of a masterpiece.

I hope you know that it also speaks volumes about you.

The things people said about you when you were growing up—what your mom may have said or your dad, grandparents, or siblings—they don't matter. The things your teachers said or your friends and neighbors said don't matter. Were you always blamed for trouble or consistently ignored, dismissed, or overlooked? It doesn't matter. Regardless of the way others have viewed you, my friend, God has already said what you are: You are His workmanship. You are His masterpiece. Where others see a block of marble with flaws and jagged edges, God sees the treasure within.

He sees you.

He sees that you are "fearfully and wonderfully made" (Psalm 139:14).

You Are Named

Artists and sculptors who create masterpieces give their creations names that reflect their meaning and purpose. You also have a name. It points to your purpose, your destiny. Your name expresses the divine reason for your existence.

Scripture tells us that one day, those who overcome will receive new names. Each one will be known only to the one who receives it.

> He who has an ear, let him hear what the Spirit says to the churches. To him who overcomes, to him I will give some of the hidden manna, and I will give him a white stone, and *a new name* written on the stone which no one knows but he who receives it (Revelation 2:17).

To be given a new name assumes that a name has to already exist. You have a name on earth. Your name reflects your purpose, destiny, and divine reason for being. It could be your given name, a spiritual name, a nickname, a title, or some other name that best reflects you.

To better understand the significance of a name, consider some names in the context of biblical cultures. In biblical times, a name involved more than nomenclature. Instead, a name frequently indicated the nature, purpose, and makeup of the individual. For example, Abraham means "the father of many," and Joshua means "Yahweh is salvation." A name often determined the expectations for what a person would become. Sometimes a person's name was changed to better reflect his or her purpose on earth, as when God changed Jacob's name to Israel. Do you know your name? If not, ask God to show you. Ask Him to reveal the name that defines who you are, because God has named you.

You Are Known

You are not only named but also known by the One who names you. A masterpiece is frequently known in connection with its creator. We listen to Handel's *Messiah* or Beethoven's Fifth Symphony. We look at Michelangelo's *David* or Monet's *Sunflowers*. A masterpiece is rarely known simply by its own name but also by the one who made it—the master of the piece. As a child of God, you are uniquely created by Him. He desires to be connected to you, and He wants others to know you in connection with Him. He wants those who see you to say, "I know her—she's God's Sarah," or "I know him—he's God's Matt." "There goes God's _____." (Fill in the blank. You are known by your connection with Him.)

You Are a Masterpiece

As a masterpiece, you are rare, special, valuable, named, and known in connection with your Creator. But this brings a challenge. Satan does not want you to know that you are a masterpiece with a divinely ordained destiny because if you do, you will view yourself in a new way. You will naturally change the way you plan, think, walk, talk, dress, dream, treat others, treat yourself, and act.

And ladies especially, please remember that a masterpiece is often protected in highly guarded settings so that people who walk by won't feel free to touch it, grab it, or put their hands all over it. A masterpiece is so valuable that it is touched only by the one assigned to care for it—the one who knows how to handle it in a way that respects and retains its beauty and worth.

You are a masterpiece. A painting. A poem. A song. A statue. A work of art.

Think of yourself that way. Embrace yourself that way. Honor yourself that way. In so doing, you are honoring Him who made you.

Now, I can hear you saying, "But, Tony, I don't feel like a masterpiece." And that's okay because I'm not talking about your emotions right now. I'm talking about you. Imagine someone who is African-American saying, "But I don't feel African-American." Or someone who is white saying, "I don't feel white." Those feelings are real, but in a sense, they are irrelevant because they don't change the facts.

You are a masterpiece whether you feel like one or not.

You may feel like a failure, but God says you are His workmanship, created in Christ Jesus for good works. That's the reality you need to focus on when your feelings tell you something else. God will raise your feelings up to your destiny; don't lower your destiny down to your feelings. Every day, recite to yourself what God says about you. This is one of the most important things you can do until your feelings catch up to the facts.

Functioning like a Masterpiece

You can help yourself begin feeling like the masterpiece you are by functioning like the masterpiece you are. God created you for a purpose. He didn't create you just so you could look good in the mirror, turn heads, stimulate minds, make a lot of money, or make people laugh. He gave you your gifts, personality, and strengths so you can fulfill your calling. You are created for good works. You are here to fulfill your destiny.

You will not fully realize how masterfully you have been made until you begin fulfilling your destiny because that is when you will experience the fullness of who you are. In other words, you will feel like a masterpiece when you function like a masterpiece. Likewise, as long as you can be kept from functioning like a masterpiece, you can be kept from feeling like one.

> You will feel like a masterpiece when you function like a masterpiece.

The Westminster Shorter Catechism begins by addressing a foundational need in all of us, and that is to identify why we are here. It asks, what is the chief end of man? And then it gives the answer: Man's chief end is to glorify God and to enjoy Him forever. How do you glorify God? One way is to fulfill His intended purpose for your life.

Jesus acknowledges this. "I glorified You on the earth, having accomplished the work which You have given Me to do" (John 17:4). How did Jesus glorify God? By completing the work God sent Him to do. The same is true for you. You bring glory to God as you walk in His intended purpose for your life and fulfill it. You glorify God when you choose to live out your destiny—intentionally pursuing the works God has prepared for you.

Fortunately, you don't have to carry the burden of creating your destiny. No statue, painting, or song ever had to create itself. God has already determined the destiny for your life. Your job is to walk in it.

When we looked at Ephesians 2:10 earlier, we saw that you were "created in Christ Jesus for good works, *which God prepared beforehand.*"

Anyone who has worked with me knows that I love to approach things from the end and work my way back. I like to uncover the bottom line first and then take steps backward in the planning and discussion to see how we will get there. Sometimes that proves to be a challenge, but it is the way I like to function.

The book of Isaiah reveals that God provides the supreme example of starting at the end of something and working backward to make sure it actually happens.

> Remember this, and be assured…
> Remember the former things long past,
> For I am God, and there is no other;
> I am God, and there is no one like Me,
> *Declaring the end from the beginning,*
> And from ancient times things which have not been done,
> Saying, "My purpose will be established,
> And I will accomplish all My good pleasure" (Isaiah 46:8-10).

God works from the end back to the beginning. This is similar to the way a carpenter builds a house. He doesn't start nailing pieces of wood together and hope that he eventually comes up with a house. No, first a designer determines what the house will look like. Measurements are included, along with a plan that shows where critical components will be placed, such as wiring, plumbing, and ducting. Only when the carpenter can see the finished work on his blueprint does he begin digging the foundation and ordering the materials.

When God says He declares the end from the beginning, He affirms that He has already completed a spiritual blueprint of what you are to physically accomplish. He knows your destiny. His goals for you are already set. His desires for you have already been determined. He has already dreamed His dream for you. Now He is simply rolling back through time, empowering you to cooperate by walking in what He has already prepared in advance.

> God has already completed a spiritual blueprint of what you are to physically accomplish.

We see this play out in Scripture all the time. God gives the end result to a person—we call it a vision—and then strengthens that person to walk in it. He told Moses that He was going to deliver the Israelites through him, but Moses had to take the steps in order to do it. He told Abraham that he would be a great nation, but Abraham had to get busy with Sarah, despite their ages or how they may (or may not) have felt. He told Nehemiah that the walls of Jerusalem would be rebuilt, but Nehemiah had to ask his king for a leave of absence in order to do what God had declared would be done.

God's purposes for you are already complete. He has already blessed you with "every spiritual blessing in the heavenly places in Christ" (Ephesians 1:3). Your blessings are already there. The victory is already won. Your destiny already exists. If you aren't feeling like a person of destiny, you probably have not yet started to function as a person of destiny.

If you will grasp the truth that you have been intentionally created in Christ Jesus for good works that God has already prepared, it will change your life. It will change the questions you ask. Instead of trying to figure out everything, you only have to figure out one thing: What is God's plan for you? When you focus on that, you will walk in what God has already prepared for you.

God has been to the end and back again. He has the blueprint of the house. Now He asks only that you walk with Him by faith as He builds the house with you. You don't need to fix it. You don't need to force it. You don't need to construct it. You don't need to arrange it. You don't need to maneuver in order to get it. But you do need to follow God's direction and walk in it.

A Masterpiece like No Other

Unfortunately, though, many of us try to live out other people's destinies instead of our own. That is why so many Christians live unfulfilled and unsatisfying lives. They pursue destinies that were never designed for them. They see someone else's destiny and like it so much that they try to make it their own. But God hasn't equipped you to fulfill someone else's destiny. He has a destiny just for you. You will never be completely satisfied until you are fulfilling your own destiny.

What is your destiny? The choice is not yours to make. Instead, it is a reality that is yours to discover. For example, an appliance doesn't choose what it will do. A refrigerator doesn't decide to refrigerate. A stove doesn't decide to heat. The manufacturer makes that decision. And if a refrigerator tries to heat, you will find a completely ineffective refrigerator, and everyone who tries to use it will be frustrated. The refrigerator would be trying to function outside of its intended design.

Friend, God has a purpose for you. He has a divinely ordained purpose just for you. It includes various things, such as your passion, your personality, skills, dreams, and hurts. All of these merge together to empower you to fulfill your destiny.

Your destiny is *the customized life calling God has ordained and equipped you to accomplish in order to bring Him the greatest glory and achieve the maximum expansion of His kingdom.* Keep in mind that your purpose isn't just about you. It's about God and His kingdom agenda.

And another thing—your destiny may be closer than you think. It is not far away in an obscure location, hidden until you find it. Neither is it something you will dread having to do. The apostle Paul explains that your destiny is in you already. "It is God who is at work *in* you, both to *will* and to *work* for His good pleasure" (Philippians 2:13).

> Your purpose isn't just about you. It's about God and His kingdom agenda.

God is already working in you, giving you both the desire (the will) and the direction (the work) to live out your destiny. You already have it. You don't need to go searching for it. The closer you get to God and the more you are able to discern His voice and leading in your life, the closer you are to living out your destiny. It's already in you.

You have already chosen to take an important step toward discovering and living out your destiny by exploring what God's Word says on the matter as we look at it together throughout these pages. I high-five you, fist-bump you, and applaud you for that, and I'm eager to go on this journey with you. Nothing is more exciting than to see someone truly enter, own, and experience his or her destiny. I want that for you. Let's roll.

Kingdom 2

I'm an American because I was born in America. I was born in Baltimore, Maryland, and at the moment of my birth, I immediately qualified to be an American citizen. My birth determined my citizenship. As an African-American, my roots are not from here. My roots run deep two continents away. Regardless, I am a citizen of America because this is where I was born.

Being born in America affords me all of the rights, privileges, and protections given to American citizens. Yet even though I was born here, my experience of the American dream is not guaranteed. My birth only gives me the opportunity to pursue the American dream. Not pursuing the American dream does not take away my citizenship. However, it may take away my ability to fully enjoy and maximize the benefits of my citizenship.

If you are a part of the family of God, having trusted the Lord Jesus Christ as your personal Savior, you are a citizen of God's kingdom because you have been born again. You have been birthed into God's family, thus affording you access to all of the rights, privileges, and protections that come from His throne. But even though you have been born into the kingdom, you may or may not be enjoying or maximizing the benefits of the kingdom. If you don't pursue all that you can do in the kingdom, you won't lose your citizenship in the kingdom, but you most certainly will reduce your experience of the benefits of the kingdom.

First Things First

God's kingdom agenda can be defined as the visible manifestation of the comprehensive rule of God over every area of life.

Frequently in Scripture we read that Jesus came to preach the gospel of the kingdom of God. In fact, Jesus's longest sermon in the Bible is specifically about the kingdom. The centerpiece of that sermon is located right in the middle of it. There Jesus definitively explained how we are to view and position God's kingdom in our lives. This principle is the foundation you will build on as your destiny takes shape.

> Seek first His kingdom and His righteousness, and all these things will be added to you (Matthew 6:33).

I want you to focus on the word *first*. If that word gets lost in your life, your experience of God and His plans for you will be diminished. God and His kingdom demand to be *first*. God does not demand to be one among many or one of your top priorities. He says we are to seek Him *first*.

The problem in most of our Christian lives, and the reason why so many of us are not fully experiencing and living out our destinies, is that God and His kingdom are not first. Sure, He's there. He's in the vicinity. He's one of the things on the list, but He's not first.

As a pastor, I have the opportunity of talking with many people about their spiritual lives, especially in the counseling context. Those who can't seem to overcome their struggles frequently tell me they just don't have time for God. My reply is always the same: "You make time for whatever is first in your life. If you don't have time for God, He is not first."

> You make time for whatever is first in your life.

When God created man, He made it clear that He wanted to be *first*. The Bible tells us that God rejected Cain's offerings, but Abel brought an offering to God of the *firstlings* of what he had. Proverbs tells us, "Honor the LORD from your wealth and from the *first* of all your produce" (3:9).

The Israelites were commanded to give the Levites, who were chosen to serve God in His temple, an offering from the *first fruits* of what they had: "You shall give him the *first fruits* of your grain, your new wine, and your oil, and the *first* shearing of your sheep" (Deuteronomy 18:4). Over and over again, God tells His people that they are to bring Him what is *first*—not the leftovers. When Jesus spoke to the church at Ephesus, He told them that they had left their *first* love (Revelation 2:4). He wasn't saying they didn't love Him, but that they didn't love Him *first*. In Colossians we read that Jesus "will come to have *first* place in everything" (Colossians 1:18).

We don't like to have other people cut in front of us when we are standing in a long line. When God tells us to put Him first, He is saying that He is tired of other stuff cutting in line ahead of Him. We thank Him for everything He has given to us, and then we allow the very things that we thank Him for to cut in line ahead of Him—in our thoughts, time, and priorities. Yet Jesus says, "Seek *first* His kingdom and His righteousness." This is not a request or a suggestion. It is not something God hopes you will consider. This is the nonnegotiable reality that you must live out in order to fully realize and experience the greatest manifestation of your destiny.

God is not one among many. He is to be *first*.

Let God Be God

Most homes include living rooms. Yet in my opinion, the living room has been misnamed. The living room is typically just a visiting room. More often than not, we live in the kitchen, den, or bedrooms of our homes, not in the living room. In fact, when I was growing up in Baltimore, I would often be told to stay out of the living room because it was set aside for visitors. I recently visited my parents in Baltimore, and they still had plastic on the furniture in this so-called living room—which is rarely lived in.

Just as we have misnamed the living room, many of us have misnamed God. We call Him our God, but we're only visiting. We pop in on a Sunday or maybe a few times during the week. We sit through a visit with God rather than living out a first-place relationship with Him. Yet God says we are to seek Him first. If that reality and priority is missing in your life, you have just identified the reason why you have not yet realized your destiny. If you acknowledge God as God and yet don't treat Him as God, you cannot enjoy the benefits of His kingdom. God says to seek His kingdom first. Not second, third, fourth, or tenth.

One day, a married couple left their home for a trip overseas. They made their way to an airport, and when they reached the ticket booth, the husband turned to the wife and said, "Darling, I wish I would have brought the piano."

> If you acknowledge God as God and yet don't treat Him as God, you cannot enjoy the benefits of His kingdom.

She replied, "Why would you want to bring the piano? We don't need a piano on our trip overseas."

To which he said, "I wish I would have brought the piano because our passports are on the piano."

Regardless of what else they had, without their passports, they weren't going anywhere. They may have saved their money, planned the details, and packed their belongings, but if the passports were missing, everything else they did was in vain. They couldn't go overseas without their passports.

If you are looking for your passport to your destiny, it is in the kingdom. Seek *first* the kingdom of God.

The kingdom presumes the presence of a King. And if He is a King, He is the Ruler. Seeking first the kingdom means seeking God's rule and authority in your life. It means that when you have to make a decision, you go to Him first. When you have to resolve a problem and are looking for a solution, you go to Him first. For so many Christians, God is like a spare tire—they go to Him when they've tried everything else and it hasn't worked. The key to every success, every fulfillment, and every opportunity to overcome the challenges in your life is this one kingdom principle: *Seek first His kingdom.*

It's All About Him

Once there was a man who had two cows. He told his wife he was going to sell one cow and keep the revenue. Then he said he would sell the other cow and give the revenue to God.

The next day, the man's wife noticed that he was sad. "What's wrong?" she asked.

The man paused, considered his words, and then replied, "God's cow just died."

When you seek first your kingdom, your dreams, your desires, your plans, your programs, and your agenda, God's cow always dies first. He always plays second fiddle. If anything gives or suffers, it's likely to be spending time with Him, following Him, or pursuing His agenda. And yet you may still pray, "This is my rule, my reign, my plan, my kingdom...bless me, God." God is not going to bless the advancement of any other kingdom than His. To do so would be as ridiculous as the American government promoting the welfare of other nations to our own detriment. That would cause an uproar from those who pay the taxes.

The secret to living out the fullness of your destiny is this one word: *first*. It consists of prioritizing the rule of God and advancing His kingdom in every area of your life. You can listen to a million sermons, read a million books, and pray a million prayers, but none of that will help you live out your destiny until you put God first.

Why do so many people today who have so much access to biblical teaching continue to live defeated lives outside of their destiny? The answer is that they are living with a wrong focus. Their decisions, conclusions, desires, and disappointments are based on self-fulfillment and will. Yet anytime you start with the wrong focus, regardless of how far you go, you will always be headed toward the wrong destination.

To get to your intended destination—your destiny—you need to first and foremost make sure that you start with the right focus: God. The foundational principle for your destiny is this: God created you to put Him and His kingdom *first*.

You were created for Him. You weren't created for you.

Our church often sings, "It's all about You; it's all about You; it's all about You, Jesus." But often believers' actions sing another chorus altogether: "It's all about me; it's all about me; it's all about me, so get on board, Jesus."

God did not create you so He could spend all His time trying to figure out how to help you. God created you for the destiny He has for you—to accomplish His plan for the advancement of His kingdom and for His glory. Any other foundation than that will take you anywhere else *but* your destiny.

> The foundational principle for your destiny is this: God created you to put Him and His kingdom *first*.

Scripture tells us that Enoch walked with God, not that God walked with Enoch. God is not your copilot. He is *first*. The apostle Paul writes, "For us there is but one God, the Father, from whom are all things and we exist for Him; and one Lord, Jesus Christ, by whom are all things, and we exist through Him" (1 Corinthians 8:6).

You exist for God's kingdom. Your destiny involves His agenda. The Bible doesn't open with, "In the beginning, you..." The Bible opens with, "In the beginning, God..." God *is* the beginning.

Through Him and for Him

The book of Colossians goes deeper into this foundational truth. "By Him all things were created, both in the heavens and on earth, visible and invisible, whether thrones or dominions or rulers or authorities—all things have been created through Him and *for Him*. He is before all things, and in Him all things hold together" (Colossians 1:16-17).

Notice that it does not say, "All things have been created through Him and *for you*." God created all things through Him and for Him. That includes you. You have been created for God Himself.

Not only that, but verse 17 tells us that God is *before* all things as well. *Before* means *first*. Living out your destiny is all about proper alignment. When God is positioned first in your life, then the rest of verse 17 holds true as well: "In Him all things hold together."

If you are unraveling, if things in your life are falling apart, or if you lack peace, security, stability, and calm, the first thing you need to ask is what position you have assigned to God. If He is truly before all things, He will hold all things together. But if He is not before all things, you cannot expect Him to hold all things together. God has to be positioned before all things in order for Him to hold those things together.

Why do so many people struggle with stability, calm, and purpose? Why do they so frequently suffer emotional, spiritual, or physical chaos? The answer is simple: God has not been positioned before all things. He is not first. Instead, He is in addition to all things. Or perhaps He even comes after trying other things. Or we get around to Him sometime later. Yet God will hold the plan of your life together only when He is *before* all things in your life.

> If He is truly before all things, He will hold all things together.

Paul sheds more light on this in Ephesians:

> He made known to us the mystery of His will, according to His kind intention which He purposed in Him with a view to an administration suitable to the fullness of the times, that is, the summing up of all things in Christ, things in the heavens and things on the earth. In Him also we have obtained an inheritance, having been predestined according to His purpose who works all things after the counsel of His will (Ephesians 1:9-11).

God saved you not just so you can go to heaven—which will be great!—but so that He could fulfill His purpose through you on earth. Don't misinterpret what this means. God wants to empower you. But He wants to empower you according to His purpose, not according to your desires outside of His purpose and intention for your life. If you are living outside of God's agenda, you are missing out on the full realization of His power in your life to fulfill that agenda. You aren't experiencing God's reality within you to the maximum potential because you are building on the wrong foundation. You are starting from the wrong place.

The Purpose of God

In the Old Testament, we read about the life of God's servant David. He was not a perfect man, but he was nonetheless a man after God's own heart. In the book of Acts, we discover what that means: "David, after he had *served the purpose of God* in his own generation, fell asleep, and was laid among his fathers" (Acts 13:36).

David was about more than just church attendance, Bible reading and memorization, committee membership, and dancing in the street. David, the man after God's own heart, was a man after God's purpose.

David's biblical epitaph tells us a lot simply by what it does not say. We do not read…

"David, after he had become the head of the company…"
"David, after he had made so much money…"
"David, after he had won so many battles…"
"David, after he had risen in the social circles…"
"David, after he had purchased many brand-name clothes…"

No, instead it reads, "David, after he had served the purpose of God…" That's what it means to be a man or woman after God's own heart. David did what he had been put on earth to do. David knew that it wasn't about him. He hadn't bought into the "bless me" mentality, in which God is a cosmic vending machine—you put in your coins, push the buttons, and He dispenses what you want. No, David realized that God's blessings were tied to God's purpose. He realized that his destiny was tied to God's desires and that the blessings he received flowed out of his destiny. They were not independent of it.

For thousands of years, people believed that the sun and the planets revolved around the earth. The earth was the center of everything. It wasn't until the sixteenth century that the Polish astronomer Nicolaus

Copernicus published *De Revolutionibus Orbium Coelestium*, his treatise that presented the first heliocentric model of our galaxy.

Many believers have done the same thing philosophically and psychologically. They have gotten it all wrong. They view themselves as the center, and everything else, including God, revolves around their own lives. In fact, this has become such a prominent belief system in these latter days that we are close to falling into an epidemic of narcissism.

But that is not what God says. God says He is the center around which we are to revolve. He is the focal point. He holds all things together.

Friend, if you truly want to discover and live out the full power and meaning of your destiny, leave your vending-machine attitude behind and make God the central focus in your life.

When a woman gives birth to a baby, she must adjust to the baby. In order to fully nourish and cherish the new life she has been given, her sleeping schedule must adjust. Her schedule must adjust. Her priorities must adjust.

New life means adjustment.

The new life in you, which you were given when God saved you, necessitated an adjustment in your perspective, planning, and priorities as well. If it didn't, you are still living for you. You are still the center of your universe, and your life is not yet revolving around God's intentions for you.

A Miracle or a Mess?

When people receive the dreaded news that they have cancer, they face a bad situation. The cancer wants to take over. Cancer wouldn't be so bad if it would just stay still.

A lot of us want God to do what we want cancer to do. Show up and stay still. We want to pencil Him in for a few hours on Sunday and possibly a few prayers, a devotional book, or even a couple of chapters of the Bible during the week. We want to toss Him into a few of our conversations. But when it comes to actually letting Him take over, that's not how we want to roll. We allocate our time, talents, and treasures to accomplish our own purposes rather than God's. And because of that, we often live with emptiness or chaos. If we will only yield to God and His kingdom agenda, we will see Him make miracles out of our mess.

Yet instead, that which could have been a miracle becomes an even greater mess. Consider Lucifer, for example. Lucifer had the best destiny possible. He was appointed as Chief Angel in Charge. God created him as the number one angel. All other angels were to follow his lead for God's glory and purposes.

Before God created mankind, He created angels. Angels were God's first created order of beings. Angels are spirit beings whose purpose is to mirror God's glory back to Him. They were designed as reflectors of the glory of God.

> If we will yield to God and His kingdom agenda, we will see Him make miracles out of our mess.

We read in Isaiah 6 about the angels with six wings. With two of the wings, they covered their eyes. With two of their wings, they covered their feet, and with two of their wings, they flew. They were uniquely designed to give God the highest level of glory due Him. Not only that, but God designed and created myriads of them. Scripture refers to myriads or legions of angels. An untold enormous number of angels were created to facilitate God's purposes in His kingdom—namely, to bring Him glory.

And the angel named Lucifer was number one of all of them. He was brilliant, beautiful, powerful, and unique. If the angels in heaven before the creation of the world were like a car lot, all of the other angels would be sitting outside on the lot, but Lucifer would be on the showroom floor. He was the bright and shining star. His job was to lead the angels in praise and worship, among other things—all to bring glory to God. But of course you know the rest of the story, which includes his rebellion when he decided to establish his own kingdom.

Ezekiel tells us that his heart became proud because of his beauty and that his wisdom became corrupted because of his splendor (Ezekiel 28:17). Isaiah tells us that he asserted, "I will make myself like the

Most High" (Isaiah 14:14). Satan, then Lucifer, wanted a promotion to become ruler of his own kingdom. He didn't want to put God *first*. As a result, he lost his destiny. His beauty disintegrated into destruction. His miracle became the mess that threatens each and every day. Satan provides the strongest warning about your destiny. If you are seeking something that leaves God out, or if you are setting up a rival kingdom, you cannot expect to have God's blessing on it. God has created you for His purposes and for the advancement of His kingdom, and that is what He will support.

A popular song a few decades ago was titled, "What's Love Got to Do with It?" Many believers today are singing, "What's God Got to Do with It?"

The answer is this: Everything. When you realize that God has everything to do with everything in your life, and when you begin to put Him first in your thoughts, actions, desires, time, talents, and treasures, you will see Him manifest His glory and His plan in you.

On Display for God

My favorite place to visit is New York City. I love New York. One of the more popular stores in New York is located on Fifth Avenue. Saks offers shoppers a unique experience of high-end products in a classy and elegant environment. The busy and bustling streets of New York—filled with noisy traffic, storefront music, and people rushing about—are nothing like the quiet and serene showrooms of Saks. Yet to get people off the streets and into their store, Saks has to do something to catch their attention.

> God has created you for His purposes and for the advancement of His kingdom, and that is what He will support.

So they dress up mannequins in the best of what they have and place them in the well-lit windows lining the sidewalks. These mannequins are put on display in order to give a visual representation of the store and an invitation inside.

Friend, God has a kingdom, and it's not like this world. His kingdom offers peace, satisfaction, order, and a wonderful destiny. As His child, you have been placed in this world for a reason. When people see you, they should want to know more about God and His kingdom. They should want to come inside. You are to glow in the light of His love so much so that others will stop what they were doing, turn from where they were going, and interrupt what they were saying to take notice of this representative from another kingdom.

But you can only do that if you put God first. If the people clothing the Saks mannequins insisted they be clothed from a lesser retailer or even in their own designs, they would lose their jobs. Saks determines which clothes represent their store the best, and that's what they put in the display windows. Likewise, God promotes and blesses that which will reflect Him best. He says clearly to seek Him and His kingdom *first*.

When I was growing up in Baltimore, I enjoyed attending an Orioles game every once in a while. Baseball is always a fun sport to watch. In one game in particular, something very interesting happened. One of the batters hit what looked like an in-the-park home run. The ball hung out in the corner of left field as he rounded first base, second, and third, and then crossed home. But when he reached home plate, he was called out because when he rounded first, he neglected to touch the base.

In baseball, if you miss first base...well, it doesn't matter what you do after that. If you missed first base but went on to touch second base, third base, and even home plate, and even if everyone congratulated you when you got there, you are still out. If you miss what is first, it doesn't matter what else you do.

God promotes and blesses that which will reflect Him best.

Friend, I would like to challenge you to change one thing in your life and to watch that one thing change everything else. From this point forward, put God *first* in all of your life. Not because this is His request, but because it is His demand. He tells you that when you do, "all these things will be added to you." You will experience the fullness and maximum potential of who you are along with the blessings He has in store for you as you enter into what He has ordained you to be.

In a Fog

A swimmer named Florence Chadwick was the first woman to swim both directions of the English Channel. Early in her career, she attempted to swim the approximately 26 miles from Catalina Island to the California Coast. On this particular day, the grueling swim that stretched for miles was made even more difficult by a dense fog. After more than 15 hours in the icy cold water of the Pacific, Florence decided to quit. Unable to see her destination, she lost both the motivation and the strength to continue. Exhausted, she climbed into the boat that was trailing her. After she got in, she was asked why she had quit. Florence replied with all the fog, she didn't know how far she had to go. Less than a mile from her destination, she quit simply because she lost hope in what she could not see.

Florence was a fierce competitor at heart and did not waste the defeat. Instead, she learned from it. Some months after giving up, Florence decided to try again. On that day, the same thick fog covered the water, blocking her view of land. But she had learned from her experience and was determined not to give up. She later said she mentally pictured the California shoreline the entire time she swam. With every stroke, she saw her destination. The mental vision of her destination empowered her to reach it.

Friend, this world is just a fog. If you focus on this world, it will distort your perspective and slow your progress. It will misinform you that you are not as far along as you really are and that you are not as near to your destiny as you might actually be. Focusing on the world creates static on the line that will interfere with what the Spirit wants to speak to your mind (see Romans 12:1-2).

But if you focus your mind on God and His kingdom, you will pierce through the fog of this world. You will reach your destination victoriously. Seek Him first, and you will make it. It's a guarantee. *All* these things will be added to you—including your destiny.

Rationale 3

G od is a God of purpose. We read in the book of Psalms that He is also a God of plans: "The counsel of the LORD stands forever, the plans of His heart from generation to generation" (Psalm 33:11). Not only that, but God has a specific plan for you. Jeremiah 29:11, which we will look at in more detail in the final chapter, says, "'For I know the plans that I have for you,' declares the LORD, 'plans for welfare and not for calamity to give you a future and a hope.'"

You are here for a reason. The tragedy is that most people never get around to discovering and living out the reason why they have been placed here on earth, so they live empty, frustrated, and irritated lives.

As we explore this topic of destiny, I want to give you six reasons, or rationales, why discovering your destiny is critical. You may wish I would skip this part and just get to the nitty-gritty of how to find your destiny. But I can't tell you how to find your destiny until you are first convinced that you need to find it. So I want to set the stage by considering why living out your destiny is so crucial. Living out your destiny addresses six key areas in your life: fulfillment, direction, stability, significance, identity, and provision.

Fulfillment

All of us struggle with various issues or challenges in our lives. But one of the dominating issues that plagues many of us today is a lack of fulfillment. Jesus tells us in John 10:10, "I came that they may have life, and have it abundantly." An abundant life is a life that is not void, or empty. It's life as it was meant to be lived—full and satisfying. It's full of meaning.

Conversely, a lack of fulfillment is one of the major reasons people commit suicide or couples get divorced. Other individuals turn to coping mechanisms to fill this void within them, such as working too much, spending too much, partying too much, popping too many pills, or drinking too many drinks. The inner emptiness that pervades many people's lives today exists due to a lack of personal fulfillment in relationships, career, spirituality, or other aspects of life.

Friend, a lack of fulfillment directly correlates to a fuzzy sense of your destiny. If you do not know your destiny or are not working toward it or living it out, you won't feel fulfilled simply because you won't have tapped into the most authentic, genuine part of who you are. Anytime you have to rely on artificial sources of happiness, energy, enthusiasm, passion, vision, and the rest, you are not utilizing and maximizing the rawest part of you. Nothing can replace living the way you were created to. Nothing can measure up to truly living authentically according to your very own unique destiny. Everything else may satisfy for a moment or at the surface level, but it will not satisfy you deeply and abundantly in your very core, where true fulfillment lives.

> A lack of fulfillment directly correlates to a fuzzy sense of your destiny.

Some people think they will find their fulfillment climbing the corporate ladder. They think they will find it in the world's definition of success. But tragically, when they get to the top, they discover that the ladder was leaning against the wrong wall.

Far too many people are living unfulfilled lives simply because they have not tapped into their unique reason for being, their own personal God-given design, their destiny. They cannot say, "This is who I am. This is why I am here. This is why I exist." Until you can say that, you will struggle to find fulfillment.

Why? Because success is not doing more of something than others have done or doing it better than they have done it. Success is doing what you were created to do. You are successful when you have carried out *your* purpose, not when you have carried out someone else's purpose, and not when you have carried out what someone else wants your purpose to be.

Neither is success about money. Not that having money is wrong—it's not. But having money is not the same thing as being successful because money is temporal, and your life is not. You are eternal. You have probably seen the bumper sticker that says, "He who dies

> Success is doing what you were created to do.

with the most toys wins." Of course, that's a lie. It should read, "He who dies with the most toys dies." Regardless of how many toys you leave behind, dead is still dead. Life isn't about what you accumulate this side of eternity. It is about what you accumulate for eternity.

Jesus offers you abundant life. But to have that life, you need to connect with the eternal purpose He has for you. In Him and His will, you will discover true and lasting fulfillment.

We shouldn't be completely satisfied with worldly success because it can never bring us true significance. Fulfilling your destiny answers the question of your significance.

We have a large number of singles in our church, and I have noticed a difference between miserable single people and fulfilled single people. Those who are fulfilled are living out their destiny. If you are single but are not living out your destiny, you are likely to wrap your whole life around someone who you think will complete you. On the other hand, when you know who you are and why you are here, you will have an answer for the question of your significance.

Direction

Have you ever seen middle-aged people who are still trying to find out who they are? Nothing is wrong with changing majors while you're in college, but if you're a middle-aged adult and haven't yet discovered or uncovered your purpose, you have some work to do. Knowing your purpose will give you direction so you can arrive at your intended destination.

Paul wrote about direction to the church at Corinth. "I run in such a way, as not without aim; I box in such a way, as not beating the air" (1 Corinthians 9:26). In other words, he was not just out there somewhere aimlessly going around in circles. Paul had a clear direction for his life. Therefore, he was able to get to his intended destination and fulfill his destiny.

On my iPhone is an app called Maps. In Maps, I can input my present location and any destination, and the app will instantly display a route that will get me there. However, if I opened up Maps and indicated my current location but then failed to type in an intended destination, the app could not provide a response when I pushed the Route button. Without a destination, Maps cannot respond with directions. It cannot provide me with a route if I do not tell it where I'm planning to go.

After you board an airplane but before you take off, the flight attendant or the pilot will announce where the flight is headed. They will confirm the intended destination. If you ever find yourself on a flight to St. Louis but you planned to go to San Francisco, you need to disembark for one simple reason: The pilot is going to St. Louis whether you want to or not. If you are on the wrong flight, you are the one who must adjust and get off because the pilot's flight plan and destination are set.

Friend, if you do not know where you are headed, you cannot know the route or the flight plan that will get you there. Rather than going through life with an intended destination, you will bounce here and there like a ball in a pinball machine. You'll be trying this, that, and the other thing, hopeful that one will lead you to a good place. Rather than take the straightest available path to your destiny, you will meander. Anyone who has wandered aimlessly knows that a lot of time is wasted by roaming here and there.

When we live without direction, we can't be clear about how to make decisions. Life is filled with ambiguity. Should you take that job?

Should you move there? Should you date that person? Or marry that one? Should you volunteer in that capacity? Should you spend your time in that manner?

Direction matters, and knowing your intended destination will help you answer those questions wisely. Without a clear sense of direction, life is hit and miss.

Stability

A clear sense of your destiny makes your life stable—circumstances no longer control your emotions or your decisions. If you are not clear about your purpose, you are prone to being blown about by situations. If something difficult or challenging comes up at work, you may want to throw in the towel and quit. Or if someone has a bad day and acts or talks in a way that he shouldn't, you might never want to talk to him again. You can count on one constant in life: Something is always going to go wrong. Challenging circumstances will always arise. The question is, what are you going to do in the face of those circumstances? Are you going to give up, or will you endure them with a positive outlook because you know you are on the path to your destiny?

When you are clear about your purpose, you will not allow circumstances to dictate your decisions. That doesn't mean you won't sometimes feel discouraged, disappointed, or irritated. Rather, it means your decisions will be guided by your purpose regardless of how you feel. And fortunately, when you begin to act on those decisions and fulfill your purpose, your feelings will soon catch up as well.

> When you are clear about your purpose, you will not allow circumstances to dictate your decisions.

Paul is an excellent model of stability through a firm sense of purpose. Paul was one of the most abused men in the Bible. In his second letter to the church at Corinth, he talks about shipwrecks, hardships, beatings…one mess after another. But after Paul lists the difficulties that would have caused most of us to up and quit, he says, in essence, "I'm fine." He says that because he is living out his eternal purpose in Christ, he doesn't lose heart (2 Corinthians 4:16). Paul remained stable in spite of the instability all around him because he knew his destiny and was committed to fulfilling it.

In his letter to the church at Rome, he speaks of tribulation, distress, peril…but then he wraps up his long list of negative and challenging circumstances with this confident statement of stability: "But in all these things we overwhelmingly conquer through Him who loved us" (Romans 8:37).

At first glance, Paul seems to be contradicting everything he had just listed. But he was saying that his position, his destiny in Christ, overruled his circumstances.

When you are living out your destiny, even on your worst day, you still have a purpose, and you are still intent on pursuing and fulfilling it. You are in the center of what God wants you to do, so you keep going. Destiny gives you stability, and stability fosters endurance.

Significance

Lois (my wife) and I were in Italy not too long ago, and one of the museums we visited displayed many of Michelangelo's unfinished works. This museum held piece after piece of incomplete statues. Some of them showed only an arm or a foot or a shoulder. Some were almost finished, and others were barely begun. As I walked through this museum looking at statue after unfinished statue, I began to think about heaven. Many of us are going to get to heaven one day and stand before God without having fulfilled our purpose. We will be like one of those unfinished statues because we never allowed God to chisel out His complete design in us.

Michelangelo's other pieces are displayed prominently in the most elite museums around the world, but what remained undone wound up in an obscure museum in Italy. It was akin to a freak show of art simply because these unfinished pieces never reached their potential. Lacking significance, they remained unnamed, unclaimed, and compared to the finished works, unseen.

Friend, you are significant. You matter. Your destiny matters. God has a plan for you that not only affects you but, as with all blessings, touches others as well.

You may not feel significant. You might prefer to be different from the way you are—another gender, another height, another race—but God purposefully made you the gender, race, and height you are. God has arranged or allowed all of the experiences in your life—the good, the bad, and the bitter—to help facilitate your destiny. You are who you are so you can fulfill your destiny. That's why you are the gender you are and the race you are. It's why you have the intelligence you have—for your destiny.

You are significant. Don't let the culture's assessment of significance keep you from being chiseled into the magnificent work of art God intends you to be. Who knows what unfinished work might have received even more acclaim than Michelangelo's *David* had it been completed? Who knows what masterpiece remains imprisoned in a block of stone with its significance hidden from sight?

Discovering and fulfilling your destiny unleashes your full significance for all to view.

Identity

All of us are vulnerable to a terrible crime—identity theft. We receive warnings about it on television routinely. You probably receive offers in the mail that promise to keep your identity safe. People commit identity theft when they pretend to be you and use information about you to access your resources without your permission. They want your Social Security number, your credit card numbers, and other information that will enable them to steal from you.

People wreak havoc when they rip off your identity. Often, before you determine what has happened and can stop it, the thief has already destroyed various aspects of your life. The thief can steal your money, put you in debt, and mess up your credit rating. By ripping off who you are, thieves can get access to what you have.

Identity theft has a parallel in the spiritual realm. The evil one seeks to steal what God has ordained for you. He rips off your identity. In John 10:10, Jesus states clearly, "The thief comes only to steal and kill and destroy; I came that they may have life, and have it abundantly." The thief wants to steal and destroy that which Jesus came to give—life. Satan wants to ruin your life by confiscating your identity in Jesus Christ.

People spend a lot of time and energy today trying to discover who they are. They go on quests seeking to somehow find themselves. The problem is that our identities have already been messed up by so many things. Some of us were raised in situations that distorted the way we think about ourselves and others. Some of us have had negative experiences with people—friends, spouses, coworkers—that have affected the way we perceive who we are. The media is constantly inundating us with new definitions of ourselves. In fact, many people are so confused about their identities that they will pay professionals hundreds of dollars to tell them who they are.

You know you have lost touch with your personal identity when you spend time wishing you were someone else. If you are doing that, either you don't know who you are or you don't think much of who you are. People will spend a lot of money dressing up, hoping their looks will bolster their identity. If they hear someone say, "You're pretty" or "You're handsome," they feel as if they are someone. But like a mannequin in an upscale department store, you can look good but still have no life. You might simply be positioned on stage for a moment without ever living out your destiny in the abundant life Jesus Christ came to give.

This problem with personal identity has caused a tremendous amount of chaos in our world today because people spend a large amount of their time, money, and energy searching for who they are. But if you don't know who you are, and you begin searching for your identity, how will you know when you find yourself?

The New Creation

Paul tells us in his letter to the church at Corinth exactly who you are as a believer in Jesus Christ.

From now on we recognize no one according to the flesh; even though we have known Christ according to the flesh, yet now we know Him in this way no longer. Therefore if anyone is in Christ, he is a new creature; the old things passed away; behold, new things have come (2 Corinthians 5:16-17).

When Paul says "we recognize no one according to the flesh," he is saying we do not evaluate things merely by their external, physical appearance. That is not the criterion by which we evaluate others, nor is it to be the criterion we use to evaluate and know ourselves. Rather, we want to know and understand the essence—an individual's (or your own) authentic core.

Because you are a believer in Jesus Christ, your authentic core is a brand-new creation. You have been re-created in Jesus Christ. He didn't simply perform a repair job on your sinful self; He placed a brand-new essence inside you. A butterfly is not a patched-up caterpillar. Neither is it a caterpillar that had some surgery or work done on it. A butterfly is a brand-new creation that has come from the caterpillar.

Each of us has a brand-new creation inside us. But we can't force it to come out, and we can't use it to patch up or fix what we have. No, we experience the newest and truest form of our own personal destiny by abiding in Jesus Christ.

> Because you are a believer in Jesus Christ, your authentic core is a brand-new creation.

What would you think if a butterfly could talk, and it said, "Well…really, I'm just a caterpillar." You would probably think it is one confused talking butterfly because it is not a caterpillar any longer. Yet as long as the butterfly identifies itself incorrectly, it won't experience its own destiny to the fullest degree.

Your identity determines your future. In other words, if you define yourself inaccurately, you will function improperly.

When two men first meet, they often ask each other, "What do you do?" This question is common simply because men are often defined by their work. They attach their identity to what they do. That is why retirement is often difficult for professional athletes. Many will go into deep depression because the thing they had poured their lives and identities into for so many years is now gone. They have to rediscover who they are because their sport was their identity. They had been defined by their function.

Yet Paul says we are not to look at each other or ourselves that way. Within each of us is a brand-new creation. Too often, too many voices are telling us who we are, and too many things are seeking to define us. Yet God is the one who is to define us. Paul tells us this as he continues in his letter to the church at Corinth: "Now all these things are from God" (2 Corinthians 5:18). When he writes "all these things," Paul is referencing what he had just stated—"New things have come." He is referring to the new creation. You are no longer defined by the old things that have passed away, but rather by the new things that have come from God. If you want to know who you are, you must let Him tell you because He is the One who has given you the new things in your new creation.

> You are no longer defined by the old things that have passed away, but rather by the new things that have come from God.

When you tie your identity to the old you, you define yourself by flawed sources, including your own opinion of who you are. That is why we experience so many messed-up relationships—we bring the old mess into the new relationship. If your dad told you what it meant to be a man or a husband, and he was messed up, then your understanding of what it means to be a man or a husband will be messed up as well. The same is true for daughters and mothers.

The surest way to destroy any opportunities for living out your destiny is to be confused about what it means to be the best you that you can be. Functioning according to the flesh, which has been flawed by sin, circumstances, history, and all sorts of other things, will sideline you and keep you from your destiny.

You may not be living out your destiny right now because you have been defining your identity by the flesh rather than by the new creation placed in you through Jesus Christ. In Acts 17, Paul gives us an idea how comprehensive this reality is.

> The God who made the world and all things in it, since He is Lord of heaven and earth, does not dwell in temples made with hands; nor is He served by human hands, as though He needed anything, since He Himself gives to all people life and breath and all things; and He made from one man every nation of mankind to live on all the face of the earth, having determined their appointed times and the boundaries of their habitation, that they would seek God, if perhaps they might grope for Him and find Him, though He is not far from each one of us; for in Him we live and move and exist (Acts 17:24-28).

God has determined your appointed times and boundaries. He has set your destiny in motion. He has created something new within you, and you can locate your destiny by connecting to Him. "In Him" you live and move and exist. Your true identity comes from abiding in God and fulfilling that which He has destined you to do. In other words, when you discover who He is, you will discover who you are. If you ignore who He is in you, you will never fully discover who you are. As a result, you will live your life in trial and error as you attempt to somehow locate yourself.

Imperishable Seed

You discover who you are when you discover who He is as He operates in you. You discover who you are when you recognize the new creation inside you. When you trusted in Jesus Christ for your salvation, God deposited His life inside you in spirit form. He deposited His living seed. We read in 1 Peter, "You have been born again not of seed which is perishable but imperishable, that is, through the living and enduring word of God" (1 Peter 1:23).

Your new identity in Christ was placed in you in seed form. James writes about this seed that came through the word of God: "In humility receive the word implanted, which is able to save your souls" (James 1:21).

The new seed planted in you when you were saved came with the potential for growth. In order for that seed to realize its destiny, it needs to grow. For example, if a watermelon seed does not grow, it will never reach its potential of being a watermelon. Or if an acorn never grows, it will never be an oak tree. Many believers are not living out the truest manifestation of their destinies because the seed of the new creation within them is not growing. Yes, they attend church, read their Bibles, and practice a number of spiritual activities, but their destiny is in the seed. It is not in the activities. The DNA of your destiny has been planted within you, and the only way to live it out is for the new creation within you to grow. The life of Christ must be made manifest in your own life.

Let's say I am holding a watermelon seed in my hand, and I want to see it grow so I can have some watermelon. So I decide to pray over my watermelon seed: "Father, O great Creator of watermelons, I have a seed in my hand, and I am asking You to do something with this seed so that I can have some watermelon. Please."

After I pray this prayer, I recruit a number of other people who will join with me as I hold my watermelon seed and pray the same prayer again. So we join hands and pray.

After we pray, I decide we are going to open up our Bibles and read what Scripture has to say about how God created the plants of the earth and how He created this watermelon seed. We gather together and read our Bibles.

After we read our Bibles about the watermelon seed, I decide to take my watermelon seed to church and set it on the very first pew in the front row, and I preach over that watermelon seed, telling it that I want it to become a watermelon.

When all is said and done, I have prayed over my watermelon seed, read what my Bible says about my watermelon seed, and brought my watermelon seed to church. Yet nothing has changed with my watermelon seed because I performed religious activities without placing my seed in the soil. In order for that seed to grow, it has to be positioned in soil that will enable its growth.

Abiding

Your new creation, the new seed planted within you, will grow in the soil of a relationship with Jesus Christ in connection with His Word. This is called *abiding*. To abide with something means to hang out with it or to loiter around it. In order to truly experience all that God has prepared for you, you need to hang out with the One who holds your destiny in His hands.

In the book of John, Jesus tells us one of the secrets to achieving our destinies: "Abide in Me, and I in you. As the branch cannot bear fruit of itself unless it abides in the vine, so neither can you unless you abide in Me" (John 15:4). When your identity is connected to Jesus Christ and the new life He has planted within you, you are able to carry out all that God has for you to do. Jesus continued, "If you abide in Me, and My words abide in you, ask whatever you wish, and it will be done for you" (verse 7).

> Your new creation, the new seed planted within you, will grow in the soil of a relationship with Jesus Christ in connection with His Word.

Christ in you provides the soil for your seed of new life to be nourished and grow. When you abide in a relationship with Jesus, you don't have to force yourself to develop, and you don't have to make things come together. With the right seed in the right soil and the water of the Word, you will grow into your destiny.

Provision

Lastly, God's provision is directly tied to your destiny. God always provides for what He destines. If you are not experiencing His provision, consider whether you are walking in your destiny. God is not obligated to provide the things you need to reach a destiny of your own making. He is obligated to provide only for the destiny He has designed you to fulfill.

When Jonah boarded a ship to Tarshish, running from God and from God's purpose for him (preaching in Nineveh), he had to pay his own fare. Jonah had to foot his own bill. He had to cover himself. Such is the case when you or I venture away from God's purpose for our lives.

God's provision for Sarah and Abraham was clearly linked to His purpose for them. God told both of them that His purpose for their lives was to produce a son. That son would be the channel through whom God would bless all of humanity. Yet Sarah and Abraham didn't see how God could come through on His promise. They couldn't figure out how God would provide, so they assumed He couldn't provide. Because of this, they took matters into their own hands, and Abraham had a child with his wife's maidservant, Hagar.

Had Sarah and Abraham placed their faith in God's promise and His ability to provide for that promise, the Israelites would not have had to experience all of the chaos that came through Ishmael and his descendants.

On the other hand, centuries later, Elijah took God at His word and trusted in His ability to provide for the calling He had given him. One day God used ravens to deliver food to Elijah; another time He provided through a widow at Zarephath. Even though God provided through various sources, Elijah was faithful to do what God had purposed, knowing that God would provide for him along the way.

God will provide everything you need to do whatever He has called you to do—financially, emotionally, and spiritually. Keep your eyes open for His provision because it doesn't always come the way you might expect. He has a purpose for who you are to be and what you are to do, and as you live out that purpose, He will provide all that you need in the most helpful way.

———■———

Discovering and living out your destiny are crucial because they address your needs for fulfillment, direction, stability, significance, identity, and provision. When you get clarity on your calling—when you have a clear picture of your purpose—you will also receive all you need to carry it out. God may not always call the equipped, but He always equips the called. He will equip you with all that you need—spiritually, mentally, emotionally, relationally, financially, and more—when you live out your destiny.

Completeness

4

Many Christians today are living decaffeinated lives. The energy, zest, and power seem to be gone. Or rather, these believers are like hamsters on a wheel—ever moving yet never arriving, spending their days, evenings, weeks, months, and years in endless and meaningless cycles.

Have you ever hopped in the car and gone for a Sunday drive? I'll admit, I enjoy driving. I don't mind taking a trip across the country or from Dallas to Baltimore to visit my parents. But getting in the car just to spend time driving around with no intention of going anywhere...well, that is difficult for me to fully enjoy. My dad used to take the four of us kids and my mom on Sunday drives. They quickly got old because we had no plan, no purpose, and no destination. We were going nowhere because we had nowhere to go.

Sunday-drive mentalities leave far too many Christians living without a sense of significance, feeling as if they don't matter simply because they have not discovered how they matter.

As we saw in the first chapter, your destiny is the customized life calling God has ordained and equipped you to accomplish in order to bring Him the greatest glory and achieve the maximum expansion of His kingdom.

To live without fulfilling your destiny is to be similar to the Dead Sea in Israel. It exists, but nothing can live in it. No fish can swim in it.

Nothing can grow in it. In fact, you can't even swim in it. The best you can do is float. Its shore is 1388 feet below sea level—the lowest land on the planet—so water runs into it but nothing flows out of it.

Far too many people are living Dead Sea lives with no outlets and no flow. They suffer perpetual stagnation because they have lost sight of the value of fulfilling their destinies. Or changing metaphors, far too many people spend a lot of time making a living but not a lot of time making a life. Because of this, they suffer from what I call the same-old disease.

Every day you get up from the same old bed and go to the same old bathroom to look in the same old mirror at the same old face. Then you go to the same old closet and put the same old clothes on the same old body. After that you eat your same old breakfast at the same old table and then get in your same old car to go to your same old job. After working all day next to the same old people for that same old pay, you get back in your same old car and drive on the same old road back to the same old house. Later, you pick up the same old remote, sit down in the same old chair and watch the same old shows until you go to the same old bed and wake up the next day to rehearse the same old routine.

Far too many people settle for a common life rather than an extraordinary life.

Don't misunderstand me. I'm not saying that anything is wrong with having a routine. Rather, I'm saying that something is wrong if your routine isn't tied to your destiny. Unfortunately, for many people, the routine is tied solely to existing and not to their destiny. They have tried to determine their own destiny rather than seek God for the destiny He has for their life. As a result, they lack the power to bring Him glory and cooperate with Him in the expansion of His kingdom. Over time, this leads to frustration and disappointment. Finally, they quit trying, quit hoping, quit believing.

> God's power is tied to God's purpose.

God's power, however, is tied to God's purpose. It is not tied to what you want your purpose to be or think it ought to be. Walk in

His purpose, and you will have His power. Walk in your own, and you won't.

A Created Destiny

No manufacturer designs and builds a product and then asks that product why it was made. The created thing cannot tell the creator what its purpose ought to be.

I assume that as you read this, you are either wearing a pair of shoes or will wear a pair of shoes sometime today. If you were to ask your shoes what their purpose is, would they tell you? No. The shoe designer can tell you why they were made.

Sometimes people can't find their destiny and their calling because they are trying to tell themselves why they have been called. They are trying to self-define their own calling. But keep in mind that a calling always assumes a caller. If your phone is ringing, someone else is calling you. You are not calling yourself.

Understanding that God is the caller and you are the callee is one of the foundational steps to living out your destiny. God is the designer and you are the design. God is the Creator and you are the created. That means you can never discover your destiny apart from God. It is impossible.

Many families experience conflict today because the family members don't know their destiny. Whenever you put frustrated or disappointed people in the same home and add the normal trials and tribulations of life, conflict is inevitable.

This is also the biggest difference between the successful single and the defeated single. The former knows his or her purpose, and the latter does not. Those who do not know their purpose may think that all of life is wrapped up in finding a man or a woman who will make them whole. A mate is a significant part of one's life, but unless you can offer your future mate a whole person to begin with, you will shortchange him or her in the relationship. You will seek to make that person fill a role that he or she could never fill—to give you your significance.

If you are single, your future mate may be "all that and then some," but he or she is not God. He or she is not your Creator. And he or she does not determine the destiny God has for you.

God says in the book of Jeremiah, "Before I formed you in the womb I knew you, and before you were born I consecrated you; I have appointed you" (Jeremiah 1:5). God doesn't say, "Before your future mate formed you in the womb…"

God formed you. God knew you. God consecrated you. And God has appointed you. Your destiny is tied to your Creator.

A Customized Destiny

God not only creates your destiny but also customizes it just for you. No one else has your destiny—only you. Once you realize that, you will see the foolishness of trying to be someone else. Why would you want to be someone else anyhow? God already has one of that person. If you become another one, God doesn't have one of you.

What's more, you will never feel more alive than when you are carrying out the destiny specifically designed for you. Even though I am in my sixties now, when I preach, I still feel young enough to take on the world. A church member once told me that I come alive when I step into the pulpit. (I trust that wasn't just a nice way of saying I'm boring when I'm not in the pulpit.) I am fully alive there because I am fulfilling my destiny.

> You will never feel more alive than when you are carrying out the destiny specifically designed for you.

In fact, before I ever had a church, I would do anything I could to fulfill my destiny. From the time I was 18 and God called me to preach, you could find me anywhere and everywhere preaching. Sometimes I would climb onto the back of a parked car or a truck so my voice would carry better, and I would start preaching to anyone walking by. You could also regularly find me at bus stops, preaching to people as they got off the bus.

I didn't mind being harassed from time to time—even once by the police. I didn't care because I knew my calling. I didn't know many sermon topics at the age of 18. Basically I had one sermon: Repent and be born again. But I preached that same sermon over and over again because, as Paul wrote, "Woe is me if I do not preach the gospel." My calling was and is the fire in my bones that propels me to preach.

Friend, if you do not pursue and live out your destiny, you will spend your entire life wishing you were someone else and trying to be someone you are not. If you are not happy with who you are, you have not yet discovered who God created you to be.

Like your fingerprints and your DNA, your destiny is uniquely yours. That truth ought to influence the way you view and respond to situations and events.

The biblical story of Esther is about a beautiful woman. God used Esther's beauty and her background to accomplish His destiny for her life. Because of her beauty, Esther was chosen by King Ahasuerus as his new bride. Yet once she moved into the big house, the evil Haman made a plot to commit genocide against her people. Nonetheless, Esther had apparently become so accustomed to her new luxurious way of life that she didn't feel like risking it in order to help her people. Esther's cousin Mordecai remedied the situation by reminding her of her purpose.

> Do not imagine that you in the king's palace can escape any more than all the Jews. For if you remain silent at this time, relief and deliverance will arise for the Jews from another place and you and your father's house will perish. And who knows whether you have not attained royalty for such a time as this? (Esther 4:13-14).

In other words, "Esther, your move uptown had a purpose, and it wasn't just about getting you out of the hood. Being pretty had a purpose, and it wasn't just about you falling in love. God put you in a strategic position at a strategic time to fulfill a strategic purpose that entails more than just shopping and customizing your wardrobe."

Esther was to look at her life in terms of her destiny, not merely in terms of her money, status, image, house, and relationships. She was to consider her reason for being in connection with God's kingdom and His agenda.

People who are serious about fulfilling their reason for being placed on earth will learn to consider all of life with God's intentions in mind. That worldview will then impact their decisions.

A Comprehensive Destiny

My daughter Chrystal loves to put together puzzles. As a child, she frequently spent hours putting together complex puzzles. Today, as a wife and mother of five, she still does puzzles when she can find the time.

Having just one piece of a puzzle doesn't do any good. A puzzle is incomplete with only one piece. The piece belongs to something much larger and more comprehensive than just itself. Without the larger part to which it belongs, the one piece loses its significance.

The same holds true for many believers today. Many Christians are living with feelings of insignificance because they cannot see how they relate to the much larger, comprehensive puzzle of God's purpose. You may be a fancy piece, a pretty piece, a handsome piece, or a well-crafted piece, but until you connect to the greater meaning for which you were created, you are just a piece without a picture.

And as we have seen, this is the greater meaning: God has created us all to bring Him the greatest glory and achieve the maximum expansion of His kingdom through the impact of our good works. Good works are biblically authorized activities that benefit people for time and eternity and that give the credit to God. If you are a Christian, whatever you are called to do will achieve both of those things. God's kingdom is His comprehensive rule over all of His creation. Fulfilling your destiny includes doing the kind of things that manifest the presence of God to a greater degree.

> Fulfilling your destiny includes doing the kind of things that manifest the presence of God to a greater degree.

Every Christian is a part of God's kingdom and a piece in God's puzzle of life. Advancing God's kingdom isn't only for professional ministers or evangelists. It is for everyone. As a child of the King, you have been "rescued…from the domain of darkness, and transferred…to the kingdom of His beloved Son" (Colossians 1:13). That means that everything you do has now become kingdom activity, even if you once considered it to be secular. There is no distinction between the secular and the sacred when you are a kingdom-minded person. Everything is sacred for those who are living underneath the overarching rule of the King in His kingdom.

If you are a mother and you are washing dishes for your family, you wash them sacredly. If you are a widget producer and you are producing widgets for your company, you produce them sacredly. "Whether, then, you eat or drink or whatever you do, do all to the glory of God" (1 Corinthians 10:31).

My doctor is Kenneth Cooper, "the father of aerobics." Dr. Cooper was recently recognized at Harvard University with the Healthy Cup Award for "dedication to understanding the scientific link between exercise and good health." One day, as I was sitting in Dr. Cooper's office and he was fussing at me the way he normally does, he began to tell me the history of how his dream—to create a place that promotes preventative medicine through good health and fitness—came into being.

"People think this is my job, Tony," he said. "They don't understand that this is my calling." Dr. Cooper went on to tell me that he is not a medical doctor simply because he enjoys medicine. He chose to be a medical doctor because he was called by God to work in medicine. Medicine is his ministry. Roughly only 100,000 people jogged in 1968 when Dr. Cooper first published his bestselling book *Aerobics*, which introduced the word and the concept to the American culture. Now, four and a half decades later, that number exceeds 30 million. Those 30 million people are being strengthened in order to have a better opportunity to fulfill their destinies.[2] God is using Dr. Cooper's calling in connection with countless other people's destinies as well. His piece is part of a larger puzzle. Dr. Cooper's puzzle piece is significant due to his widespread recognition and impact, but like him, every person has a purpose to fulfill that links with the greater goal.

A few years ago I was visiting Dr. Billy Graham, and while touring his facilities before sitting down with him, I met a young woman who performed data entry at the ministry. When I asked her about her job, she told me she had been doing it for years. With a smile from ear to ear, she said, "I love what I do."

Confused how someone could love sitting at a computer all day entering and double-checking names, I asked her the obvious question. "Why?"

Without a moment's hesitation, she replied, "Because this is my calling. God called me to use my computer skills to expand Dr. Graham's ministry. When I enter a name in the computer, I know that this is someone who has been led to Jesus Christ through one of our outreaches. Or when I create lists for sending out booklets and follow-up information, I know that I am helping people who have just come to the Lord."

I have run across very few people in my life who understood and grasped the importance of their purpose the way this woman did. She did not merely perform data entry. She performed data entry for a greater purpose—to glorify God and expand His kingdom.

Whether you are a homemaker, doctor, janitor, lawyer…whatever God has called you to do will have eternal repercussions. When you view what you do through that lens, you too should smile from ear to ear because you will understand that what you do matters in the larger picture of life. You are a piece of God's puzzle. Your destiny is directly linked to others in His kingdom.

> Whatever God has called you to do will have eternal repercussions.

If you are a kingdom person fulfilling your destiny, those around you will be impacted by your kingdom worldview. When this happens, you will discover that you are a part of a greater, comprehensive significance that includes confiscating the spoils of hell and transferring them into the realm of heaven.

Intention

5

I know a man named Billy who lives in a nearby town. Billy is what you might call a junkyard specialist. He spends his time at local junkyards looking at things other people have thrown away. He searches through the junkyards for valuables that other people have deemed worthless.

Billy then loads his treasures into his truck and hauls them back to his garage. In his garage, he turns what was once considered junk into contemporary art pieces. He then sells his art pieces to interested buyers for upward of $5000 each.

Billy can do this because he sees more than everyone else does. When Billy looks at junk, he sees a masterpiece in the making.

Friend, as we have seen, you are a masterpiece. You may feel worthless, used up, or discarded. But when you met Jesus Christ, you met the One who can transform you from what you think you are into what you truly are—a valuable masterpiece with a purpose.

Billy's artwork does more than adorn homes and decorate rooms. It has a unique way of starting conversations. When people look at one of Billy's works, they often ask the owner to tell them the story behind it. The owner then explains how Billy went about crafting the marvel. In other words, Billy's art brings him glory.

Similarly, you are to be a conversation starter about your Creator. You are here to bring Him glory.

Satan wants you to lose sight of your value and purpose, but God wants you to embrace it. He wants you to display it. He wants you to be the conversation starter that reflects His glory. And yes, that even includes the nicks and dents and that which others may deem as worthless. In the hands of the Master, it all works together to create something of utmost value—you!

Chance or Purpose?

So many people today believe in chance rather than God, who controls the universe. Your view of God's sovereignty affects your view of your destiny. If you don't believe that God created you on purpose and that He works all things together for good when you are called according to His purpose, you will believe that events and circumstances happen by luck. But in fact, God sovereignly allows those things to happen for His purpose. Still, if you do not connect them with His purpose, they have no meaning for you.

As a result, you end up living your life as a cosmic lottery rather than as a response to a sovereign God who put you here for a reason. You cannot have God and chance. The two are incompatible.

How does this relate to purpose? Just as the things going on around you do not happen by chance, neither are you here by chance. God created you on purpose. You are not the result of random forces in the universe coming together. Neither are you a mistake. Every part of you was intentional.

> O LORD, You have searched me and known me.
> You know when I sit down and when I rise up;
> You understand my thought from afar.
> You scrutinize my path and my lying down,
> And are intimately acquainted with all my ways.
> Even before there is a word on my tongue,
> Behold, O LORD, you know it all.
> You have enclosed me behind and before,
> And laid Your hand upon me.

Such knowledge is too wonderful for me;
It is too high, I cannot attain to it (Psalm 139:1-6).

After setting the relational scene between himself and God in these verses, David narrows his focus to his own creation.

You formed my inward parts;
You wove me in my mother's womb.
I will give thanks to You, for I am fearfully and wonderfully made;
Wonderful are Your works,
And my soul knows it very well.
My frame was not hidden from You,
When I was made in secret,
And skillfully wrought in the depths of the earth;
Your eyes have seen my unformed substance;
And in Your book were all written
The days that were ordained for me,
When as yet there was not one of them (verses 13-16).

You have been created on purpose. You are not a mistake. In fact, no one is a mistake. There is no such thing as an illegitimate child. Relationships may be illegitimate, but every child born of an illegitimate relationship becomes legitimate because he or she has been formed by God (Isaiah 49:1). Whether the child is the product of rape, a broken relationship, or some other bad situation, the child is legitimate and has a destiny. In order for that child to be born, God had to go to work. And for God to go to work, He had to intend for that child to be born.

When God formed you, He determined what race you would be. He determined what gender you would be. He determined what would make up your DNA, which would then determine your height, hair color, shape, and unique personality. God made you, *you*. He made you the person He wanted you to be. He made you special and unique when He wove you together in your mother's womb.

Think about it—if you are a mistake, God made a mistake. And if God made a mistake, He cannot be perfect. And if God is not perfect,

He is not the perfect God He says He is in the Bible, which makes God a liar.

So the next time you wonder if you are a mistake, an afterthought, or someone who has not been intentionally designed with a destiny—keep in mind that if you believe those things, you are actually calling God a liar. In order to throw away your confidence in your intentional design, you have to throw out God too.

Abortion is wrong not only because it takes away a life but also because it takes away the destiny God intended for that life, a destiny that has the potential to impact and influence others for good. Abortion removes more than one life—it removes the impact of that one life on countless others.

You may or may not be a football fan, but you have probably heard of a man named Tim Tebow. In the 2011–2012 NFL season, Tebow became somewhat of an icon. His name frequented the news and newspapers. *Saturday Night Live* even spoofed him. From students in high schools to the entire panel of sports announcers after the Broncos playoff win over the Steelers, admirers and detractors mimicked "the Tebow," kneeling as Tebow did throughout the season to give all glory to God.

But the Denver Broncos quarterback was at one time at risk of being aborted. In 1985, Tim's mother and father were serving as missionaries in the Philippines. After Tim's mother, Pam, contracted amoebic dysentery, she lapsed into a coma. The doctors, not realizing that Pam was pregnant with her fifth child, treated her with very strong drugs that caused the placenta to detach from Pam's uterine wall. This limited the amount of oxygen Tim received while in the womb.

The doctors believed Tim would be born with serious brain damage if he survived at all, and they also believed the pregnancy put Pam at high risk for further complications, so they advised her to get an abortion.

Bob and Pam Tebow refused the abortion and chose to pray for a healthy baby instead. Several months later, Pam gave birth to Tim. The rest is history. God has used Tim to be a testimony to Him on the field and off. Had Pam aborted Tim as a baby in her womb, countless people would have lost out—not just him.

When God creates a life, He has an intention for that life. He doesn't make mistakes. He is sovereign over everything, including the creation of life. This means that nothing comes to you that does not pass through God's fingers first—including your very existence. To create you, God had to sovereignly choose where you would be born, who you would be, and what His purpose for your life would be. That doesn't mean that everyone always achieves God's destiny for his or her life. Many do not seek Him, trust Him, or pursue His purpose in their lives. But God created all people with a destiny that would blow their minds if they only knew what God wanted them to do.

> When God creates a life, He has an intention for that life.

Far too often, people get hung up on things that appear to make no sense. They get stuck trying to figure out why sometimes seemingly bad things happen to good people. They fall into ruts of doubt or self-pity because they lose sight of their destiny. Without a strong faith in God's sovereignty, we can easily get sidelined and distracted from what God has put us here to do.

Keep in mind that believing in God's sovereignty does not mean you believe He *causes* everything in your life. Rather, it means that God either causes or *allows* everything in your life. And if He allows it, He can use it. Trusting in His sovereignty means trusting that He can cause everything to work toward good—even the confusing and hurtful things—if you choose to love Him and respond to Him in the calling of your destiny.

Beyond Natural

One of the greatest deterrents to living a life of destiny is a propensity to living life as a naturalist. When you live with this mindset, you do not look for the connection between the good, bad, and bitter things that take place. You do not recognize that in all of those things, God is the One who appoints, allows, and sets limitations. You do not see the meaning behind the mayhem.

If you are a woman with this mindset and cannot have a child for some medical reason, you assume that you are just unfortunate. Or if you are working hard in your career but get passed up for a promotion, you assume that you are unlucky. Or if someone buys a house you had bid on, or marries a spouse you had hoped to marry, or is born with the looks you always wanted...you assume that you missed out. When things don't work out according to your plans, a naturalist point of view can produce panic, anxiety, regret, doubt, and fear. But when you understand that God is sovereign and has created you with a purpose, you can enjoy calm and peace even in difficult situations.

> When you understand that God is sovereign and has created you with a purpose, you can enjoy calm and peace even in difficult situations.

In order to live your life calmly, you must fully embrace God's sovereignty rather than question everything. Paul experienced calm when he penned, "For to me, to live is Christ and to die is gain" (Philippians 1:21). In other words, Paul said that he could chill and accept what came his way because he knew that God was in control. He knew that God was running the show. He knew that this was God's program and that regardless of what happened, God would make the most of it.

God Is in Charge

Because God is the Creator of all things, He is in charge of all things. He says in Isaiah, "Turn to Me and be saved, all the ends of the earth; for I am God, and there is no other" (Isaiah 45:22). When God says there is no other, He is affirming that He is in charge. His purposes stand. He rules.

Consider your home. Whether you own or rent, you make the payment on your home, so it's essentially your home. Now if someone were to come into your home and start telling you to change the drapes, knock out a wall, and make all sorts of other changes just because he wanted you to, you would take one look at him and tell him goodbye—not because he wasn't being sincere, but because he was sincerely wrong to think he could come into your home and set down the priorities and rules.

This illustration is easy to understand, but the truth behind it is often difficult to live out when we apply it to God and His creation. You are His creation. This is His world. He is in charge. If you want to run your own world, go make one. But in the meantime, let God run the world He has made—which includes you. "The earth is the Lord's, and all it contains, the world, *and those who dwell in it*" (Psalm 24:1).

We experience confusion and emptiness because we try to make up our own rules in God's house. Imagine what would happen if you came to my house and started smoking or pulled out some hard liquor. Chaos would quickly ensue because I have decided that people will not smoke or drink alcohol in my home. In my home, we play by my rules.

> Let God run the world He has made— which includes you.

Many people who have been bought with Christ's blood and live in God's house nonetheless want God to adjust to them. They want God to do what they want, the way they want, when they want. And when He doesn't, they try to do it themselves. Then they wonder why they are experiencing conflict and emptiness in their lives. *Of course* you will feel distant from God and lose your sense of destiny when you do not adjust to Him. He is in charge.

Your highest calling, the most important part of your destiny, is to reflect God's glory. The primary way to do that is to align yourself underneath His rule and according to His will. Making that a priority for your life choices, thoughts, and goals will bring you closer to your destiny than any seminar, self-help strategy, or good intention ever could.

Bubba

A little over a decade ago, our church built a Christian education center. Needless to say, putting up this multimillion-dollar facility was no small feat. In fact, when the gymnasium, classroom center, and private school were finally completed, President George W. Bush attended our opening ceremony. It was a festive occasion.

However, if you had looked a year earlier at the spot where the mammoth building now stands, all you would have seen was an empty parking lot and a man named Bubba. Bubba was hired to be the foreman of the project, and as he went over the original blueprints and plans for the massive project, he told me it was the most complex building he had ever worked on. Bubba had built bigger buildings before but none that were so multifaceted. The pages and pages of drawings detailing the way everything needed to come together to make this building functional were beyond anything Bubba had seen before.

Yet despite all the challenges and the minutiae, Bubba raised up an enormous building fit to serve everyone from neighborhood children to the president of the United States.

We started out with an empty parking lot, Bubba, and some blueprints. Yet even with our human limitations and inadequacies, we were able to construct something amazing because we had a plan and the resources to carry it out.

Friend, you might be looking around your life right now and see nothing but an abandoned parking lot and a few weeds. Yet God can come into your life and connect your problems with His solutions, your needs with His provision, and your circumstances with His intentions, creating something brand-new in you. If you really want to discover your destiny, begin by embracing the truth that you were made *on* purpose *for* a purpose that lines up with God's intentions for you. If you will simply walk in the cadence of His calling, He will take what appears to be nothing and create something significant, strong, and meaningful in you.

PART 2

The Ingredients of Your Destiny

Passion

6

When our kids were younger, our family sometimes went on vacations to one of their favorite places—Disneyland. We loaded all four kids into the car and took off across the country.

While at Disneyland, we went on nearly every ride. Most of them weren't all that bad. I enjoyed myself. But one ride in particular nearly drove me stark raving mad. Maybe you've ridden It's a Small World.

On this ride, you sit on a boat and inch along a makeshift waterway through hundreds of audio-animatronic dolls singing, "It's a small world after all" over and over and over again. About midway through this ride, I wanted to jump out of the boat and swim back. It was pointless, meaningless, slow-moving torture.

Friend, if you are not fulfilling your destiny, it's a small world after all. Life loses its zest when you have nothing substantial drawing you forward. Living without your destiny is like going around and around in circles but never arriving at your destination. Life becomes a routine without any depth, drive, or meaning.

Maybe this sounds familiar to you. You may have lost your zeal for life, or what I like to call your mojo, simply because you are not functioning within your destiny. The boat of life keeps moving along slowly, and you feel trapped inside a maze of singing puppets that make no sense at all and that quickly get on your nerves.

As we begin detailing the ingredients of your destiny, I want to make clear that the number one ingredient in living out your destiny is your passion. God has given you a passion to do or to be whatever He is calling you to. There is no such thing as a destiny without a passion for that destiny. God didn't create you to do something that He didn't likewise give you the motivation and the desire to do. This motivation and desire is known as your passion.

Everyone has a passion. Even the most introverted and boring person in the world has a passion for something. People don't all have the same passion or express their passions in the same way, but everyone has passion. If you are naturally quiet and reserved, your passion might express itself through dedication, commitment, or devotion. If you are naturally more outgoing and extroverted, your passion will probably be obvious to those around you because you will pour your energy into it.

> The number one ingredient in living out your destiny is your passion.

If you are a Christian, your passion has to do with your spiritual intensity, or the fire that burns inside of you. We may not all display our passion in the same way or to the same degree, but we all have it within us. In fact, I have enjoyed basketball games or football games with friends who told me they were not emotional or passionate. But when the home team made a great play, my friends have practically knocked me over with their energy and excitement. In the right circumstances and at the right environment, even the dullest people you know will find some fire. They will discover their passion. Everyone has the potential for passion.

Yet many people don't live with their mojo or with passion because they are not where they are supposed to be. They are not doing what they are supposed to do. They have lost hope that their lives will change or have any meaning. When you look in their eyes, you can see that the life—the fire—has died out because there is nothing to burn. It is hard to have a fire in a fireplace if there is no wood on the grill. Friend, if you are not where you are supposed to be or you are not doing what you were created to do, your fire and your passion will be missing.

What Is Passion?

Spiritual passion is the God-given capacity to fervently devote ourselves to something or someone over an extended period of time in order to accomplish a goal and meet a need. Paul writes in the book of Romans about his own passion: "I aspired to preach the gospel, not where Christ was already named, so that I would not build on another man's foundation" (Romans 15:20). The Greek word translated *aspired* is *philotimeomai*, which means "to strive earnestly" or "from a love of honor to strive to bring something to pass."

Paul's aim was to "strive earnestly" to preach the gospel because it was a passion within him. It was something he needed to do. "If I preach the gospel, I have nothing to boast of, for I am under compulsion; for woe is me if I do not preach the gospel" (1 Corinthians 9:16). This echoes the prophet Jeremiah.

> If I say, "I will not remember Him
> Or speak anymore in His name,"
> Then in my heart it becomes like a burning fire
> Shut up in my bones;
> And I am weary of holding it in,
> And I cannot endure it (Jeremiah 20:9).

Jeremiah's passion to speak God's words was like a burning fire within him. That is passion. Jesus shared King David's fiery zeal, or passion: "Zeal for your house will consume me" (John 2:17, quoting Psalm 69:9). Have you ever been zealous for something that was too hot *not* to handle? Something that burned within you until you acted on it? That is a fire. That is your passion. It wakes you up at night or keeps you from going to sleep in the first place. It causes you to think about the subject when the subject isn't even on the table. Passion is a bubbling volcano in your soul. It's the very fuel of your calling and destiny. It keeps you going even when you want to be "uncalled." You know it's your passion, as I have mentioned before, because it's something you would do even if you weren't paid to do it.

Staying on the Path

Have you ever taken a job just for the money, only to later discover you had made a huge mistake? Have you ever thought you would rather be poor than have to go to work? I can't think of anything worse than knowing that for the rest of my life, I have do something I can't stand—just for the money. I'm not saying we never have to do things outside our calling or purpose. We all have to do those things. When I was attending classes full-time in seminary, I also loaded luggage on buses from eleven p.m. until seven a.m. That job was hard, backbreaking work, and it definitely wasn't my destiny. But I endured it because it helped me reach my goal and my destiny.

We all have to do that from time to time, but I would hate to spend a lifetime doing something outside of my calling. I'm a preacher. I was made to preach. I was created to study God's Word and to proclaim it. If I wasn't a preacher by trade, I'm sure that regardless of my job, I would be trying to figure out a way to preach God's Word whenever I could—during breaks, the lunch hour…whenever. Preaching God's Word is my passion. It lights the fire in me. Regardless of how tired I am, if you stick me in front of a group of people who have come to hear God's Word, I will preach like there is no tomorrow.

In fact, just this past week—within a five-day period—I will have preached eight sermons, each at least an hour long, to different groups of people. Just a month ago, I preached that same number of different sermons in two days. Some people who were with me during those two days mentioned that I started with plenty of energy and ended with even more!

> Your passion will motivate you to take steps now that prepare you to someday fulfill it.

As you move toward your destiny, you may have to do some things that don't bring out your passion. Even then you can be moving toward your passion, and that ought to serve as your motivation. So try not to feel frustrated if right now you are not doing what you were destined to do. As long as you are on the path to discovering and fulfilling your destiny, keep going. You will get there. Your passion will motivate you to take steps now that prepare you to someday fulfill it.

The only thing that can satisfy your passion is the thing that generates it. In other words, once you identify your destiny, it will create a burning desire in you, and the only thing that will satisfy that desire is to fulfill that destiny. Nothing else will do.

The Perspective of Passion

The book of Ecclesiastes was written by a very passionate man. In fact, Solomon was a player. The Bible tells us that he loved many women. He was an insatiable romantic. The Song of Solomon describes his romantic prowess. This man had passion.

In Ecclesiastes, Solomon helps us to view our passion from the perspectives of time and eternity. After Ecclesiastes 3:1-8 details that there is a time for everything, verse 11 says, "He has made everything appropriate in its time. He has also set eternity in their heart."

All of us have eternity in our hearts. We know there must be more than just what we are experiencing right now. Even people without God spend a lifetime trying to answer eternal, philosophical questions. Who am I? Where am I going? Where did I come from? They ask these questions because God has placed eternity in their hearts.

If you seek your purpose from the perspective of time rather than the perspective of eternity, life will be flat. It will lack meaning because God has set eternity in your heart. You were made for eternity. If what you are doing is focused solely on temporal results and not also on eternal results, you will be dissatisfied simply because your soul is not temporal.

Yet one ominous reality hangs over each of us on earth. Regardless of how grand or how wealthy or how successful we are, we all sense it. It is a great big neon sign over each of us that reads, "Temporary." In a sense, we are all—each of us—temporary.

Movie stars are celebrities only temporarily. They will get old, and younger people will eventually take their place. Last year's sports champion is this year's defender. Today's front-page headliner is mentioned in a sidebar on page 20 tomorrow.

Has this ever bothered you? Sometimes it bothers me. All that you accomplish on earth is temporary—if, of course, the things you accomplish are intended for and motivated by time rather than eternity. Anything that is determined by physical reality rather than focused on the spiritual reality of your soul will pass away. This is why no friendship, relationship, or even fellowship can fully satisfy you—they are all temporary, and you were made for eternity.

> You can fully maximize your life only with an eternal perspective in mind.

God has set eternity in your heart. You can fully maximize your life only with an eternal perspective in mind. Your purpose and your passion have eternity written in them if they lead you to the destiny God has given you. So the question you need to ask yourself is this: What am I passionate about that is connected to eternity?

Stirring

Frequently Scripture says that God stirred the hearts of the people He called to do something. What has God stirred your heart about? What brings out your emotions? What breaks your heart or inspires and invigorates you? What can you do or simply think about that makes you feel alive? If eternity is connected to it, that is your passion, and it will lead you toward your destiny. Pursue it. Chase it. Run after it. Go get it. Embrace it. Live it. Because without it, you will merely be existing—you won't be fulfilling your destiny.

Here's the best question to ask regarding passion: If not for the money, family responsibilities, or time, what would you do? What would that be? Do you have a secret ambition? If it is tied to eternity, that is your passion. And unless you pursue your passion, you are going to wither and die—not physically, but emotionally. Passion left unaddressed dies. When it is squelched, it goes dormant.

Seeking to Save

If you are familiar with the story of the *Titanic*, you probably already know what the greatest tragedy of that disaster actually was. Of course, the sinking of the *Titanic* was a tragedy itself. But the even greater tragedy is that most of the lifeboats were only half full.

Approximately 1500 people froze to death in the frigid waters that night when hundreds of them could have been saved had those in the lifeboats returned to rescue them. But the people who were saved got so comfortable in their salvation that they forgot that other people were dying of hypothermia. Only one of the 20 boats returned to rescue the others.

Kingdom people with a purpose shouldn't think like that. They shouldn't be thinking, "Well, I'm saved, so I hope you make it somehow too" while doing nothing for the millions of souls that are perishing. Kingdom people want to discover how they can use the opportunities and skills God has given them to provide a lifeboat for someone else. God's kingdom purposes will always involve impacting people for His kingdom. They will involve eternity. Where your passion merges with eternity, you will discover your destiny.

That doesn't mean that everyone should be a missionary or a preacher. But it does mean everyone should understand there is a kingdom operating on earth with an eternal perspective. You have a role to play in God's kingdom whether as a mother, doctor, teacher, lawyer, engineer, painter, poet, business manager, administrative assistant…

> Once you link your passion to eternity, there's no telling what God will do in and through you.

My challenge to you as you read this book is to examine your passion. Look deep within yourself and ask some strategic questions. What captures your attention? What do you think about? What do you dream of one day doing or being?

Perhaps you already know your passion. Maybe you have discovered your passion in the marketplace, but now you just need to discover how to connect it to the kingdom. You need to give it an eternal perspective. Once you link your passion to eternity, watch out—there's no telling what God will do in and through you.

Fired Up

The space shuttles were created to carry out a unique mission. They were designed to go somewhere. Yet because of gravity, the space shuttles couldn't go anywhere at all on their own—that is, until they were mounted on rocket boosters.

Before they connected with the boosters, gravity told them, "You aren't going anywhere. You are grounded." And gravity was right. But when they were in place on the boosters and the rocket engines were ignited, these earthbound multiton vehicles were able to soar.

Your passion is your fire. Yet many of us are grounded in time because of our fears. Many of us are grounded from living out our destiny because of things we've been told. We have poor self-esteem, and even though we desire to lift this mess off of the ground, we don't believe God can create enough fire. Yet if fire can lift the space shuttle all the way out of the earth's atmosphere, fire can do the same for you too.

Things move when they are fired up—including you.

Regardless of how dull you may appear or how thick your glasses are, and even if you classify yourself as a nonemotional, intellectual person, you have fire. You have passion. You may not express it the same way other people do. You may not shout, dance, or display your passion openly because we all have different personalities. But you have it. You have passion. You have that thing, subject, interest, or vision that is connected with eternity and that stirs you up inside.

If you don't yet know what that thing is, go to God and ask Him to reveal your passion to you. Ask God to light the fire within you. Ask God to show you your passion in connection with eternity so He can show you your destiny. And then hold on tight because it will be time for the ride of your life.

Vision 7

Some people suffer from a condition called myopia. Myopia, or near-sightedness, occurs when the physical length of the eye is greater than the optical length, causing the eye to reflect light inaccurately. When people suffer from myopia, they are unable to see clearly at a distance. Objects that are far away appear blurred and fuzzy. Details are lost as the sharpness deteriorates within the eye.

Myopia is frequently passed down from generation to generation. Those who suffer from myopia will often transfer a genetic predisposition toward it to those who come after them.

Unfortunately, what has happened in many people's physical vision has happened in many people's spiritual vision as well. These people struggle to see anything beyond what is directly in front of them.

We are commanded not to worry about tomorrow, but nothing is wrong with looking at it. In fact, taking tomorrow into consideration is important. The book of wisdom tells us, "Where there is no vision, the people perish" (Proverbs 29:18 KJV).

> Vision gives your destiny inspiration and direction.

Your destiny without vision is like a surgeon without a scalpel, a cowboy without a horse, or a dancer without a song. Vision gives your destiny inspiration and direction. Trying to discover your destiny without a vision is similar to trying to ignite a fire with a wet match. It won't happen. Having vision is like putting feet to your destiny or putting glasses on a person who suffers from myopia. It enables you to function more fully. It allows you to visualize things and bring them into focus so you can experience them. Your spiritual vision involves *looking further than you can physically see.*

Illumination

Before we go much deeper into vision, I want to carefully distinguish between two important concepts: revelation and illumination. God's revelation is closed. What God recorded within the canon of Scripture is complete. Nothing new is to be added to the biblical revelation (Revelation 22:18). However, God still illuminates His people. God illuminates us by showing us how His revelation (His revealed Word) applies to us. The role of the Holy Spirit is to illuminate us. The Spirit doesn't give us new revelation. Rather, He reveals what we are supposed to do with the existing revelation (1 Corinthians 2:9-13). God illuminates you by giving you a clear vision of the purpose of your life.

Keep in mind that visions bring clarity. And when you receive a clear mental picture of your destiny, you receive power. Your vision empowers you. The power comes with knowing and seeing your destiny clearly.

> When you receive a clear mental picture of your destiny, you receive power.

When your vision is clear about your future, you will make good decisions in the present—decisions that either directly relate to your vision or steer you closer to it. You will know when to say yes and when to say no. You will have a better attitude when you have to do things you don't want to do or don't enjoy doing. When you know those tasks will help you accomplish your vision, you will have more energy to do them.

A clear vision gives you power to make productive and strategic decisions. It also gives you endurance to carry out what is necessary in order to one day reach your vision. Without a vision, seemingly mundane activities really are mundane. Tasks that seem boring and meaningless really are boring and meaningless. But when God illuminates you, showing you how He is planning to use those activities to bring you to your vision, you can carry out your tasks with a renewed zest simply because you understand their purpose.

For example, this is what God said when He gave Abraham his vision:

> Go forth from your country,
> And from your relatives
> And from your father's house,
> To the land *which I will show you*;
> And I will make you a great nation,
> And I will bless you,
> And make your name great;
> And so you shall be a blessing;
> And I will bless those who bless you,
> And the one who curses you I will curse.
> And *in you all the families of the earth will be blessed* (Genesis 12:1-3).

Abraham was instructed to leave his familiar surroundings and venture into the unknown. Traveling across unfamiliar territory and terrain with supplies, people, animals, and the rest was probably not on Abraham's bucket list. More than likely, it was a long, often uneventful, and difficult journey. But Abraham had a vision that involved the promise of blessing in his future, so he was motivated to do that which most likely did not produce immediate gratification. And he was able to remain motivated for the long haul. We know this because of what the book of Hebrews tells us Abraham did in response to the vision he received.

> By faith Abraham, when he was called, obeyed by going out to a place which he was to receive for an inheritance; and he went out, not knowing where he was going...*For he*

was looking for the city which has foundations, whose architect and builder is God (Hebrews 11:8,10).

Abraham reached his destiny because he responded to his vision. He was told to go to the land God promised to show him. Abraham did not know where that land was or what it looked like, but he knew that he would find what he was searching for because he had faith that the vision God had given him would come about.

Becoming a Blessing

Based on his vision alone, Abraham set out on a path to his destiny and his blessing. Keep in mind that your destiny and your blessing will always involve others. God will work *in* you when He knows He can work *through* you. When we receive a blessing, we experience God's favor so we can extend it to others.

> God will work *in* you when He knows He can work *through* you.

Abraham made himself available as a conduit for a blessing. He set out to seek that blessing even at great personal sacrifice, and as a result, he eventually found both his blessing and his vision. Had Abraham stayed in his safe and secure surroundings with Sarah (at that time known as Sarai) and the rest of his family, he would never have reached his destiny, which was to be the conduit of God's blessings to all the families of the earth. Likewise, had Abraham decided to wait until God gave him the detailed, step-by-step road map to reach his vision, he would never have discovered and lived out his destiny.

God gave Abraham a vision. Because Abraham believed and acted on that vision as God had instructed him to, he received his blessing in full and reached his ordained destination.

Looking to the Invisible

Like Abraham, when you receive a vision, you look to the invisible. You see a picture of what will happen, though not all the details are clearly filled in. Then, when you fulfill your destiny, you make the invisible visible.

Have you ever seen an invisible coloring book? The pages appear to be blank, but when you color on them with a "magic pen," an elaborate picture appears.

This is similar to what happens with your vision. Before the creation of time, God had already established your purpose and your destiny. The image of what you will become and what you have been designed to do has already been established. Every line, color, and portion of the image is already there. But you won't get to see it or experience it until you take the "magic pen" of faith and do what God has revealed to you to do. Like a child coloring in a blank book, you may begin hesitantly. Yet as God responds to your movements by revealing more and more of your vision for you, you will be empowered to continue on in faith.

> When you fulfill your destiny, you make the invisible visible.

As God reveals your vision to you, your best response is to act on it. Take a step—God loves to hit a moving target. As you step out in response to the little He has shown you, He will show you much more. And the more you step out, the more He will show you. If you never respond to the little, you will never discover the rest. That's why Paul says, "We walk by faith, not by sight" (2 Corinthians 5:7). It involves doing something; it involves movement.

Vision involves seeing things from God's perspective. Colossians tells us that is the way we are to view life: "If you have been raised up with Christ, keep seeking the things above, where Christ is, seated at the right hand of God. Set your mind on the things above, not on the things that are on earth" (Colossians 3:1-2). When God gives you a vision, He gives you His view. He gives you an eagle eye. He gives you the ability to see tomorrow as clearly as an eagle can see the ground. You see beyond what is normal and natural. Things you have never seen before suddenly become crystal clear in your mind's eye—so much so that you might say, "I can see myself doing that" just as if you were already doing it.

You may have heard the story of a visitor saying to the director of Disney World, "Isn't it a shame that Mr. Disney didn't live to see this?" To which the director quickly replied, "He did see it. That's why it's here."

Vision involves seeing things from God's perspective.

Now, let me ask you a question: What is your vision? What do you see? If I were to ask you to write down your vision, could you do it? Or let me put it another way—when you dream, what do you dream about? What are your dreams for the next five, ten, or fifteen years? Where do you envision yourself being and what do you envision yourself doing twenty years from now? Clarifying your vision and your dream is critical because if you see only that which is in front of you right now, you will lose the momentum that comes with a clear direction. Your choices and decisions over the next five years or even the next several decades will lead you in circles rather than toward the goal of discovering, experiencing, and then ultimately maximizing your purpose. When you don't have a target, you aim for anything. When you aim for anything, you will miss everything.

A Mental Picture

Nehemiah is a biblical character who doesn't seem to get a whole lot of press these days. You don't frequently hear preachers teaching on the life of Nehemiah even though there is so much to glean from his actions and decisions. Nehemiah serves as a perfect example of someone who received a vision and responded by acting on it.

In Nehemiah's time, Jerusalem had been decimated for about 70 years. Nehemiah lived in another culture and served another king. He had very little to do with the existing status of his homeland—that is, until God gave him a vision. God gave Nehemiah a mental portrait of his purpose in relationship to Jerusalem. We know this because Nehemiah later tells us about it.

> I came to Jerusalem and was there three days. And I arose
> in the night, I and a few men with me. I did not tell any-
> one *what my God was putting into my mind to do* for Jeru-
> salem (Nehemiah 2:11-12).

Notice that Nehemiah specifically states that God put a vision in his mind. God first placed Nehemiah's calling and purpose as a thought within him. He gave him a mental picture of what He wanted him to do. God will give you a mental picture of His purpose for you. He will place within you a concept linked to your passion, skills, and desires, and then He will see what you do with what He has given you. The fulfillment of the image God originally puts in your mind is likely to be so much more than you can imagine. Had He shown you the whole picture at the start, you might not have believed Him, you might have been too intimidated to pursue it, or you might have been too overwhelmed to imagine that it could come to pass through you.

So God will often give you a mental picture that includes your vision but not in its entirety. He gives you enough for you to take the next step on the path to your destiny. But as you take that step, remember that you are heading to something that has the potential to be so much larger than what you think right now. Never let your partial understanding limit you. Sometimes God gives you only enough to get you going. If He is taking you toward something that is larger than you imagined, accept and embrace it. That happens to most of us. God often reveals only what He knows we can handle at the time.

Seeing and Feeling

Nehemiah's vision for Jerusalem came out of his burden for Jerusalem. If you turn back a chapter in his book, you will see one of the initial ingredients of his vision—his passion for his people. When Nehemiah was in Persia, his brother Hanani and some other men from Judah came from the area of Jerusalem. Nehemiah asked them how the people were faring back in his homeland. They replied, "The remnant there in the province who survived the captivity are in great distress and reproach, and the wall of Jerusalem is broken down and its gates are burned with fire" (Nehemiah 1:3).

Their response evoked Nehemiah's deepest passions. "When I heard these words, I sat down and wept and mourned for days; and I was fasting and praying before the God of heaven" (verse 4). Nehemiah didn't just hear his countrymen's report or their words, he felt them—deeply. He felt them in what I call his gizzard…that deep place inside where emotions are authentic and real.

Because Nehemiah felt the report of his fellow Jews, he did something about it. He mourned, fasted, and prayed. He sought God and His solution to a crisis and desperate situation. Nehemiah's vision was birthed out of his passion for his people, just as your vision will be birthed out of a passion that God has created within you. A burden or a passion is something that weighs heavily on you. You can't shake it easily. You can't get rid of the thought.

> Your vision will be birthed out of a passion that God has created within you.

Friend, if something on your heart burdens you or evokes strong emotions in you, before you try to talk yourself out of those feelings or rationalize them, ask God if they are clues to your vision and your destiny. Most likely they are. Passion and vision are two things that God gives you in order to motivate you for a sustained calling.

Once you jump into your purpose and start taking strides on the path toward your destiny, you will discover that not every day is a skip down the yellow brick road. Each hour doesn't bring fireworks and rainbows or exciting adventures to explore and conquer. Along the path to your destiny, you will encounter a myriad of dull moments and just plain hard work. Passion and vision are gifts from God to strengthen you and motivate you through those times. They play a critical role in helping you fulfill your destiny because they are the breath, or the wind, on which you soar. They give you strength to keep going through the tedious and the mundane.

Even when you're living out your destiny, some moments won't be filled with bells and trumpets. Your passion and your vision will often have to carry you through those everyday moments so that you will arrive at your intended destination.

Nehemiah's passion drove him to his knees. It burdened his heart so much that he went without food. He wept and called on God to intervene. He asked God to show him what to do.

What makes you weep? What keeps you up at night? What calls your name louder than food? Many of us live in a culture that revolves around food. Food is conveniently available to us in all sorts of delicious packages. In fact, food often dominates our thoughts, and our health suffers when we don't eat wisely. What burdens or impassions you so greatly that even food becomes unimportant? Have you ever been so engrossed in a project or a job or an act of service, so fulfilled and satisfied, that you lost track of time and even forgot to eat? That is passion. If that has happened to you, take note. Passion and vision are significant clues to your destiny.

Vision and Revelation

But don't let your passion and your vision lead you outside of God's revelation because if you do, you will end up on your own. Illumination is subjective, so it should always be based on revelation, which is objective. God's objective revelation is His Word. Nehemiah didn't allow his burden or his passion to go outside of God's revelation. He didn't allow his own emotions to determine his course of action. Rather, Nehemiah prayed to God using God's own words. He appealed to what God had already said. He did something that I like to call holding God hostage to His Word.

> Remember the word which You commanded Your servant Moses, saying, "If you are unfaithful I will scatter you among the peoples; but if you return to Me and keep My commandments and do them, though those of you who have been scattered were in the most remote part of the heavens, I will gather them from there and will bring them

to the place where I have chosen to cause My name to dwell" (Nehemiah 1:8-10).

Nehemiah's burden led him directly to God and His Word to look for an answer. If your burden doesn't drive you to God and His Word, it is not His vision for you. Your vision will always be connected with God Himself. His vision for you will point you toward Him.

God's Timetable

God's vision for you will also come about according to His timetable, not yours. Notice that Nehemiah concluded his prayer with a request for that very day.

> "O Lord, I beseech You, may Your ear be attentive to the prayer of Your servant and the prayer of Your servants who delight to revere Your name, and make Your servant successful today and grant him compassion before this man." Now I was the cupbearer to the king (verse 11).

God had positioned Nehemiah in a high-security position—he was cupbearer to the king of Persia. Nehemiah recognized his opportunity in light of his passion and burden, and he asked God to give him favor with the king, who could help relieve his burden. (By the way, notice that Nehemiah was working in a secular occupation in a secular environment for a secular king. God can use you wherever you are to advance His kingdom.)

Yet even though Nehemiah asked for favor on that day, God had a different timetable. Nehemiah's visitors had arrived from Jerusalem in the month of Chislev (1:1), but King Artaxerxes didn't take notice and look with favor on Nehemiah until the month of Nisan, four months later (2:1).

Nehemiah's situation shows us that we are to pray for today but to remember that God's timing is often much different from our own. Timing is everything. As God prepares you for your destiny, He also prepares everyone else who will play a part in your destiny. He lines up everything to converge perfectly at the right time. Things have to be ordered, constructed, and interlinked exactly for the right time. When that right time comes, all things will need to work together to accomplish God's purpose.

Keeping It Real

On that day in the month of Nisan, the king noticed his sadness and asked him why he was burdened. Nehemiah shared with the king from an authentic soul—his burden was real. That's one reason why your purpose is linked to passion and vision. People can say all the right things when sharing their vision, but if their communication isn't authentic, those who are listening will sense that, and they will be less likely to participate or respond. People respond to sincerity, especially when it is linked to passion and vision—just as the king responded to his cupbearer.

When Nehemiah expressed his vision and his passion for Jerusalem, he found favor. The king gave him a leave of absence to do something about Jerusalem, and he also gave him the tools, manpower, security, and freedom to carry out his vision. Nehemiah's passion and vision merged with his life situation at just the right time to lead him to his destiny.

Friend, God has a destiny for you. Discovering that destiny begins by discovering your passion. As you discover what evokes your deepest emotions and concern, notice the way God reveals that to you and how it corresponds to His Word. Seek Him. Make Him your highest passion, and He will show you your path. Make knowing and living His purpose for you your deepest burden, and He will open your eyes to your destiny.

When your passion gives birth to your vision, everything will change—your life, your decisions, and your priorities. You will experience a new fire, drive, and intentionality.

Your life is like a coin. You can spend it any way you want, but only once. Make sure you invest it and don't just waste it. Invest it in something that matters to you and matters for eternity. God has placed your destiny within you already. He wants to give you a burden and a passion to do what He wants you to do. Focus there. When you do, you will see the vision God wants to unfold in your life.

Giftedness

8

One of the greatest discoveries you can make as a believer and follower of Jesus Christ has to do with your spiritual gifts. A spiritual gift is a divinely bestowed ability that strengthens the body of Christ in order to optimally service the kingdom.

As we begin our discussion on spiritual gifts, notice the difference between spiritual gifts and talents. A talent is a human ability people have in varying levels. It benefits those who have it as well as mankind in general. You don't have to be a Christian to be talented; you just have to be human.

But a spiritual gift is much different from a talent. It is something God gives to certain individuals, and it is specifically designed to service His people and His agenda for the expansion of His kingdom. We call it a spiritual gift because it is given by the Holy Spirit and used through the power of the Holy Spirit for God's purposes.

A spiritual gift may not be something you were talented at doing before you became a believer. People often discover their spiritual gifts when they develop a relationship with the Holy Spirit. Sometimes the spiritual gift is brand-new and comes at the point of a person's salvation. Other times, God sanctifies an existing talent and transforms it into a spiritual gift.

In Christian circles, we sometimes hear people say a singer or preacher is "anointed." That term generally refers to a spiritual gift because the person is functioning beyond his or her talents or abilities. For example, Billy Graham may not be the world's best preacher in terms of technical abilities or fundamentals of oratory, but his gift, or anointing, evokes a response in people who hear him unlike any other. In fact, other preachers could recite Dr. Graham's sermons word for word, but they wouldn't receive the same response simply because they do not have the same anointing.

Some Christian musicians can sing beautifully or perform perfectly but are unable to lead a congregation in a spirit of worship. Conversely, other Christian musicians may not always sing on pitch and may not have as much experience or technical ability, but they usher people into God's presence because of their anointing, or gift. A fine but distinct line divides human performance and anointed ministry. Performance often draws attention to the person, but ministry draws attention to God, who anointed the person.

> God provides everything you need to fulfill His calling on your life.

Many Christians fail to maximize their calling simply because they are not aware of their gifts. They may be stuck trying to utilize their talents rather than seeking God for the gifts He has given them or discovering how God wants to transform their talents into gifts. Other Christians fail to maximize their calling because they don't realize they even have a gift. If you are a believer in Jesus Christ, you have at least one spiritual gift. God has equipped you with the necessary skills to fulfill the destiny for which He created you. God provides everything you need to fulfill His calling on your life. So if you are struggling with something you can't seem to do, either you are not in your calling or you have not yet discovered the gifts that God has given you and that He intends for you to use. God always prepares you for His purpose for you.

Grace Gifts

> To each one of us grace was given according to the measure of Christ's gift. Therefore it says, "When he ascended on

high, he led captive a host of captives, and he gave gifts to men" (Ephesians 4:7-8).

In this passage, Paul introduces us to the concept of spiritual gifts. He begins by clearly stating that God has given a gift "to each one of us." So if Christians say they don't have a spiritual gift, either they are actually not Christians at all or they don't yet know their spiritual endowments. If you are a Christian, you have a gift—a spiritual gift that is unique to you. Each one of us has a spiritual gift that is unique to our destiny and calling. My spiritual gift may be in the same category as yours, but it is not intended to accomplish the same purpose because each of us has a specific, personalized destiny.

After Paul informs us that each and every one of us has been given a gift, he explains that it is a "grace gift." Your spiritual gift has been given to you through grace. My spiritual gift has been given to me through grace. In other words, God gets the credit for the gifts. You and I have them because of His remarkable and unfathomable grace.

Gifts in the New Kingdom

Paul then goes on to describe the process through which this grace has been given to us. He begins by giving us the very picturesque quote, "When he ascended on high, he led captive a host of captives, and he gave gifts to men" (compare Psalm 68:18). Paul then goes into greater detail.

> Now this expression, "He ascended," what does it mean except that He also had descended into the lower parts of the earth? He who descended is Himself also He who ascended far above all the heavens so that He might fill all things (Ephesians 4:9-10).

To fully understand the impact of this passage, we need to revisit its history. At the fall of mankind in the garden, Satan convinced Adam and Eve to switch their allegiance to him. He confiscated the gifts God had intended to use for the propagation of His kingdom, and he began to use them to promote his own agenda. Satan corrupted the talents of humanity, which had been intended to promote God's kingdom, and began using them to promote hell's kingdom. He is still using them today as he tries to control our media, fine arts, schools, homes, and communities.

But when Jesus Christ cancelled the certificate of sin on the cross, He abolished Satan's authority over mankind. On the cross, Jesus began a process of taking back what Satan had stolen and using it for its original God-given purpose—the advancement of the kingdom of God.

To better understand this spiritual reality, consider a physical illustration. Imagine an army—for example, the Roman army of the first century—entering an enemy's territory and defeating its army. The conquering nation would seize the enemy's resources and use them to promote its own good. If someone had been a talented lawyer under their previous government, he now became a talented lawyer on behalf of Rome. If someone had been a talented doctor under their previous government, he now administered medicine in order to strengthen Rome. The talents of those who had been defeated were to be used on behalf of the conqueror.

In Eden, Satan seized the talents of humanity in order to promote his kingdom of darkness. He set up an enemy outpost and began to utilize the talents of humanity to promote his agenda. Yet something happened on Calvary that forever changed everything. On the cross, Jesus Christ paid the entire payment for the sin of mankind. Therefore, as a result of His death, burial, and resurrection, God put all things under His authority.

> These are in accordance with the working of the strength of His might which He brought about in Christ, when He raised Him from the dead and seated Him at His right hand in the heavenly places, far above all rule and authority and power and dominion, and every name that is named, not only in this age but also in the one to come. And He put all things in subjection under His feet, and gave Him

as head over all things to the church, which is His body, the fullness of Him who fills all in all (Ephesians 1:19-23).

Costly Gifts

Following Jesus's death on the cross, He "descended into the lower parts of the earth" and then led a host of captives to the heavenly places that He might give gifts to men. Did you catch all that had to take place? First, Jesus had to die and suffer estrangement from His Father in order to make payment for the sins of humanity. Then He had to descend in order to release and lead out the host of captives. Finally, He had to be resurrected and seated at the right hand of God in the heavenly places.

Friend, your gift did not come easily or cheaply. The spiritual gift you have received came at great cost to our Lord and Savior, Jesus Christ.

The Purpose of Gifts

As you might imagine, He gave you your gift for a purpose—to strengthen the body of Christ as it serves as His church, "the fullness of Him who fills all in all." Therefore, your gift accomplishes two things. First, it increases the impact of your ministry to the body of Christ (1 Corinthians 12:7; 1 Peter 4:10). Second, it provides a testimony of your faith to a watching world (Matthew 5:16).

There will come a day when each of us will stand before Jesus Christ to give an account for the way we used the gifts He gave us. The question won't be how much college you attended or how many seminars and workshops you participated in to sharpen your skills. No, the question will focus on how you used those seminars, workshops, and college degrees to support His body of believers and advance His kingdom of light in a world filled with darkness. How did you utilize the gifts given to you to further God's kingdom on earth? That is the question you will have to answer. If your skills and abilities did not contribute to the strengthening of Christ's church and the progression of His kingdom, then they were simply talents that never became fully maximized as spiritual gifts.

For example, if you are gifted in the area of teaching, then as a way of maximizing that gift, you are to discover how you can use your gift not only within the church but also in the culture, perhaps by teaching in a public school in order to bring Christ's light into a darkened place. Your spiritual gift ought to impact both the body of Christ and the world at large.

Paul references this dual purpose of our spiritual gifts—to strengthen the church as well as increase its impact on society.

> He gave some as apostles, and some as prophets, and some as evangelists, and some as pastors and teachers, for the equipping of the saints for the work of service, to the building up of the body of Christ; until we all attain to the unity of the faith, and of the knowledge of the Son of God to a mature man, to the measure of the stature which belongs to the fullness of Christ (Ephesians 4:11-13).

Spiritual gifts are designed to empower the church, and the church's job is to spread the kingdom of Jesus Christ. Specifically, verse 12 tells us that the gifts are given "for the equipping of the saints for the work of service." I know of no other way to interpret that statement than to say that we—the saints—have a job to do. That job is to build up the body of Christ so that the body of Christ can spread the kingdom in society.

Your Work of Service

Many Christians operate under the belief that preachers, missionaries, Christian musicians, and others who work in the church are the only ones who have "spiritual" jobs. But God has given each saint a gift in order to build up His body. The church where I pastor has a requirement for those who want to become members—they must agree to serve in a ministry of the church. This is not simply a way to recruit volunteers for the various ministries. Rather, it holds believers in our membership accountable to utilize their spiritual gifts.

I've seen many individuals in our church discover their spiritual gifts through the process of serving. Many of those have gone on to use those gifts professionally—gifts these believers previously didn't even know they had. They are now strengthening the church as well as utilizing their gifts in the society as salt and light in a world in need.

Your work of service is essential because God is bringing His whole family to a unity of the faith and to a mature man, as we read earlier. Your spiritual gifts include you—your personality, passion, goals, skills, and more—but they are not just for you. God gave you your spiritual gifts so you can be a blessing to others. If that blessing ends with you, God cannot continue to bless and maximize His work in and through you. As I mentioned previously, blessings are always intended for people to enjoy and to extend God's favor in their lives. Your gift is meant to bless others.

> Your work of service is essential because God is bringing His whole family to a unity of the faith and to a mature man.

Gifts Offer Clarity

When believers intentionally develop and use their spiritual gifts, the effects are enormous.

> As a result, we are no longer to be children, tossed here and there by waves and carried about by every wind of doctrine, by the trickery of men, by craftiness in deceitful scheming; but speaking the truth in love, we are to grow up in all aspects into Him who is the head, even Christ, from whom the whole body, being fitted and held together by what every joint supplies, according to the proper working of each individual part, causes the growth of the body for the building up of itself in love (Ephesians 4:14-16).

When believers function according to their gifts, they make decisions with clarity and aren't confused by "deceitful scheming" or "every wind of doctrine." Clear decisions create productive actions on behalf of the church and those in it. In addition to that, people flourish and grow when the whole body is fitted and held together and each member uses his or her own gift.

One night I got out of bed, and in the dark, I stubbed my toe against a table. Maybe you can relate. Now, I knew my toe was hurt because the nerves in my toe sent a signal to my brain. My brain immediately sent another signal to my vocal cords, and I let everyone in the house know I had just stubbed my toe. At the same time, my brain was telling my right hand to reach down and grab my toe. Also at the same time, it told my left foot to support all my weight as I picked up my right foot. In a split second and without even thinking, my body parts all went into immediate action because they function as a unit "by what every joint supplies." They function as a body. And that's what God calls the church—a body. We are to function together in order to impact the lives of those around us as effectively as possible.

Your Personality Profile

Several factors can help you determine your spiritual gifts, including your personality. Your personality is the part of you that makes you the person you are. Just as no two people have exactly the same thumbprint, no two people have exactly the same personality.

Your personality makes you who you are. We often refer to it as your soul. Your soul is comprised of three parts: your mind, your emotions, and your will. It is your essence—much more so than your body. When you die, your body will remain on earth and eventually decay. However, the real you, your soul, will go either to heaven or to hell, depending on whether you have trusted in Jesus Christ for the forgiveness of your sins and your salvation.

Even though everyone's soul is made up of the same three components (mind, emotions, and will), people don't express what goes on in those components the same way. Some people are introverts. They may think deep, complex thoughts or feel strong, powerful emotions, yet they do not express them openly. Then there are extroverts—most people know what they are thinking or feeling before they even enter the room! Each of us is different from everyone else because each soul (or personality) is unique.

Friend, God gave you the personality you have because it fits perfectly with the destiny He has planned for you. If you have to become somebody else in order to fulfill a certain purpose, then God wants somebody else to do it. That's not your purpose or your destiny. God made your personality to fit your destiny. Your destiny has been designed to flow with you.

Take a look at several of the personalities in the Bible. Peter was the impetuous, self-proclaimed leader and spokesperson. He was always putting his foot in his mouth and speaking whatever came to his mind. God used Peter's personality to empower him to fulfill his destiny—to announce the public beginning of the church. Paul, on the other hand, was a studious thinker. God used him to write much of the theology in the New Testament. John was the loving and intimate personality who liked to lean his head on Jesus and have a relationship with Him. God used John to write about the power of abiding in Christ (John 15) and the importance of loving relationships (1 John 3–4).

> God made your personality to fit your destiny.

Throughout Scripture, God used people's personalities to help them fulfill their destinies. God's calling is consistent with how He made you. You don't need to change your personality to pursue your destiny. In fact, a healthy awareness of who you are and how God made you will give you insight into how He wants to use you.

> A healthy awareness of who you are and how God made you will give you insight into how He wants to use you.

Several tools can help us along our path of personal discovery. One of them is a personality test called the DISC test. No personality test can sum up everything about everyone, but looking at who we are and how we function is often intriguing and enlightening.

Your destiny will include your spiritual gifts as well as your personality. One of the surest ways of finding and fulfilling that which you were designed to do is to honestly examine who God made you to be. This will take some effort, but it's worth the investment. You are a unique person whom God desires to use to bless others and advance His kingdom.

Experience 9

Life has a way of serving up a variety of situations. Some are good, some are bad, and some are bitter.

Things aren't always good. But thank God that things aren't always bad either. Still, sometimes things get even worse than bad, and those are the things that leave us with a bitter taste, a residue of undeserved or unfair pain.

The good experiences in life produce positive benefit. They are productive and enjoyable.

The bad experiences include times when you have done something wrong that has damaged a situation, yourself, or others. If you could roll back the hands of time, you wouldn't choose to make the same life choice again. Perhaps you made a mistake, committed a sin, or suffered a failure.

The bitter experiences leave their mark on you, often through no fault of your own. Someone else caused something to happen in your life—maybe he or she mistreated you, neglected you, abandoned you, or used you. In a sinful world, we run into bitter experiences or bitter people almost by the minute. Unfortunately, hurting people often turn around and hurt others, causing a cycle of bitterness to continue.

Why do some people successfully live out their destinies while others aimlessly check off each day? The difference is often the way they view their life experiences. Successful people view them all—the good, bad, and the bitter—through the lens of purpose. These individuals realize that God is able to use all of it for His calling on their lives. Aimless people and bitter people cannot see the thread that connects their life experiences to their own destinies. These people's hearts grow hard, their guilt piles high, and they are unable to move forward in life.

> Successful people view all experiences—the good, bad, and the bitter—through the lens of purpose.

The way you manage or mismanage your past experiences has a big impact on your future. Learn from your past, but don't live in it. Satan keeps you from moving forward by getting you to keep looking back. Are you the product of a dysfunctional family? God can use that for good. Did someone abuse or mistreat you? God can use that for good. Were you passed up for a promotion after years of dedicated service? God can use that for good. Has your marriage failed, did your dreams come crashing down, or did someone you trusted betray you? Did you make some decisions as a teenager that are still affecting you decades later?

God can and will use everything in your past for good—the good, the bad, and the bitter—if you let Him. Resist the tendency to grow hard-hearted and bitter. Move past your past. God wants to use the good, the bad, and the bitter to lead you into your destiny.

The Good

The apostle Paul is the foremost spokesperson for Christianity. Nobody can compete with Paul. He is the official theologian of the church. He wrote the church's constitution, the book of Romans. In fact, he wrote 13 of the 27 books in the New Testament. God could have just zapped him his great ability, but instead, God used some things in Paul's background to facilitate his mission to spread the Christian faith. God worked through Paul not only spiritually but also academically.

In the book of Philippians, we find Paul's résumé. As you may know, a résumé is important because it links your past performance to your future potential. A résumé tells where you have worked and what experiences have shaped you into the person you are. Most of us have a résumé that demonstrates continuity in our lives.

A résumé not only tells where you have worked but also highlights your commitment and faithfulness. It tells how long you have worked where you have worked. A résumé that lists new jobs every six months is not going to be a positive addition to your job interview. It implies that employers cannot depend on you for a long period of time.

A résumé says a lot. But most of the time, people try to put the best things they have done on their résumé. That's what Paul did on his résumé. Keep in mind that Paul's résumé includes items that predate his conversion to Christ.

> If anyone else has a mind to put confidence in the flesh, I
> far more: circumcised the eighth day, of the nation of Israel,
> of the tribe of Benjamin, a Hebrew of Hebrews; as to the
> Law, a Pharisee; as to zeal, a persecutor of the church; as
> to the righteousness which is in the Law, found blameless
> (Philippians 3:4-6).

Essentially, Paul says that no one had more to brag about than he did. When bragging about human accomplishments, he was at the top of the list. In stating that he was circumcised on the eighth day, he was affirming that his parents were highly religious because they kept the Old Testament law. Paul was telling us that he was raised right. He showed his parents' deep commitment to start him down the right Jewish path. His résumé began with a strong home.

He then said he was a part of the nation of Israel, meaning that he was from the nationality that was uniquely blessed by God. He was born on the right side of the tracks. He also told us he was from the tribe of Benjamin, indicating that he was from the right class in the right nationality. The tribe of Benjamin was one of only two tribes that remained faithful to God when the kingdom split in two. Paul summed this up stating that he was a "Hebrew of Hebrews." In other words, he was a super-Jew. In urban American language, Paul might have said, "I'm Jew and I'm proud."

To be a Hebrew of Hebrews meant that Paul was special. He went to the best schools, achieved the highest marks, and quickly rose to the top. Some commentators believe he had even been a member of the Sanhedrin, the ruling council.

All those things could be classified as good things in Paul's history. And God used those experiences to prepare Paul for what He wanted him to do. When God looked for someone to lead the church, write the theology for the church, debate religious leaders who opposed the church, foster the cause of Christ both academically and socially—someone who could go uptown to Caesar at Rome and who could also go downtown to the people who hurt the most—God found a man whose résumé included items He could sanctify and use to fulfill His purpose.

To sanctify something is to set it apart for God to use. Paul experienced a lot prior to his salvation that God would later use for His purposes, and God can do the same with you. He can sanctify your past experiences in business, personal achievement, worldly success…God can sanctify all of it to lead you to your destiny.

> God can sanctify your past experiences to lead you to your destiny.

Before you were saved, or before you dedicated your life to pursuing God and His purpose for you, God already recognized the experiences you needed in order to fulfill your destiny. The things you had going for you back then—God still may want to use them today. The training you received, the family you were raised in, your employment opportunities…God had a purpose in all of it. Now God wants to sanctify those experiences and use them as you fulfill your destiny.

Paul had all the raw ingredients and experiences God wanted to use. As do you. He had a purpose for that degree, education, training, job, relationship, mentor, success, and everything else that shaped you for good. God wants to sanctify the very best of your experiences and use them in your destiny.

The Bad

We might expect God to use our good experiences for His purposes, but we might wonder how a holy God could possibly use our mistakes, our failures, and even our sinful choices for His good.

One of the greatest things about God's grace is His ability to turn a mess into a miracle. I'm not saying God endorses mistakes or failures or that He accepts sin. He doesn't. Nevertheless, God can use our mistakes and failures to better equip us to reach our destiny.

We've seen how God used Paul's good experiences for his purpose. Next I want to take a look at my favorite person in the Bible, Peter. Peter is my favorite because he was always running his mouth. He always wanted to be in charge. He wouldn't let anyone else talk, lead, preach, or appear more devoted than he was. Peter was always out in front, trying to take control of the situation.

> God can use our mistakes and failures to better equip us to reach our destiny.

But sometimes Peter's mouth got ahead of his feet. In fact, Peter even went up against Satan, and he lost—big time.

> Simon, Simon, behold, Satan has demanded permission to sift you like wheat; but I have prayed for you, that your faith may not fail; and you, when once you have turned again, strengthen your brothers (Luke 22:31-32).

Jesus Christ predicted Peter's failure. Yet even though the words came from the Lord Himself, Peter thought he had everything under control. His response speaks to his own naïveté: "Lord, with You I am ready to go both to prison and to death!" (verse 33).

Peter didn't accept Jesus's prediction. He didn't own up to his own frailty. He told Jesus that he was the man. He could be depended upon. He was Jesus's mainstay—so much so that he would even die before denying Christ.

To which Jesus quickly replied, "The rooster will not crow today until you have denied three times that you know Me" (verse 34). Which is exactly what happened. Three times Peter denied even knowing the same Lord he had hours before claimed he would die for.

God allowed Peter to get in this mess, and He used it to better equip Peter for ministry. Jesus had already told him why: "Strengthen your brothers." We create some messes, make some mistakes, and commit some sins simply because of our own weaknesses, flaws, or rebellion. Yet God allows us to fall into some because He knows that when we come back, we will be stronger—our perspective will be deeper and our commitment will be truer. At times God allows Satan to trip us up so God can teach us something about ourselves and about Him.

Scripture tells us that when the rooster crowed and Peter became aware of his own sin, he wept. Failures don't get much worse than that—denying the Lord after you publicly said you would die for Him. Peter denied Jesus openly. But after he did, his repentance bore fruit in his heart. It produced an authentic humility that someone as strong willed and capable as Peter needed in order for God to use him to reach thousands.

> God allows us to fall into some mistakes because He knows that when we come back, we will be stronger.

When we repent of our bad experiences, God uses them to make us stronger. He doesn't excuse them, and He doesn't remove the consequences, but He is bigger than our failures.

God didn't turn His back on Peter because of his sin. In fact, He did just the opposite. God made sure Peter knew that He was still there and that He still cared. The angel at the tomb specifically said when speaking about Christ's resurrection, "Go, tell His disciples *and Peter*..." (Mark 16:7). "Don't forget Peter," the angel said. "I know he's blown it. I know he's betrayed Jesus. And that's why I'm calling out his name—so that he will know God wants him to know He still cares for him."

The angel singled out Peter to assure him that his denial would not destroy his destiny. God had a plan and a purpose for Peter. In fact,

Jesus singled out Peter for ministry, as we read in John 21. Jesus cooks Peter breakfast over a charcoal fire—just like the one Peter stood by when he denied knowing Jesus—and lets Peter know that He still has a plan for him. Despite Peter's failures, God still had a purpose for him, just as God has a plan and a purpose for you. Despite your failures, mistakes, and sins, God calls your name. Listen, and you will hear it. He still has a blessing to give you and a destiny for you to fulfill.

Buildings sometimes implode. They collapse, leaving a mess to clean up so the rebuilding process can begin. Sometimes the same thing seems to happen in our lives, but the hope of your Christian life is that Jesus Christ can turn the rubble and the ashes into something new.

Peter had promised to never forsake Jesus, but the rooster still crowed. Friend, when does a rooster crow? A rooster crows early in the morning, at the beginning of a new day. If the rooster has crowed after a night of your failure, that just means the sun is coming up and you can start again. The Bible is full of men and women who failed and yet discovered their destiny as God used them greatly—people such as Moses, Abraham, David, Sarah, Solomon, and Rahab.

You may have failed, but you are not a failure. That is not who you are. In Christ, you are a new creation. God can use yesterday's mistakes to strengthen you for a brighter tomorrow. Seek God in your mess. Let Him know that you are not proud of it, you wish you could undo it...but since it is there and done, you want Him to turn it all around and use it for good.

> You may have failed, but you are not a failure.

God can use the bad for good. Let Him. Make yourself available to His grace and to His mercy. He has a plan for you.

The Bitter

More than any other account in the Bible, Joseph's story illustrates how God can use the bitter things in your life to get you to your purpose. The bitter things are the situations you didn't cause and couldn't control. Rather, someone or something negatively affected you in some way.

Joseph was born into a dysfunctional family. His father, Jacob, was a trickster from birth. Some of his brothers were murderers, and one had an affair with his father's wife. Another had an affair with his own daughter-in-law. A reality show about Joseph's family probably couldn't air during prime time. It would be too dicey even for today's viewers.

Joseph was the eleventh son of twelve boys. His problems began when his brothers realized that his father loved him the most. "Now Israel loved Joseph more than all his sons, because he was the son of his old age" (Genesis 37:3). Jacob (or Israel, Joseph's father) didn't hide his favoritism at all. In fact, he broadcast it by giving Joseph a lavish, multi-colored coat.

As you might expect, this made Joseph's brothers jealous. To make matters worse, Joseph had a dream and shared it with his brothers. In it, his family bowed down to him. Rather than sit around and wait for this dream to come about, the brothers decided to kill Joseph.

One brother, Reuben, stood up for Joseph and intervened, asking his brothers to fake Joseph's death and throw him in a pit instead. The brothers later sold Joseph as a slave to a Midianite caravan heading for Egypt.

If anyone knew what it was like to be treated unfairly, Joseph did. His brothers left him for dead, lied about him to his father, and sold him into slavery. Joseph may have dragged a grudge along with his ball and chains on his way to his new destination.

In Egypt, things got even worse for Joseph. He was sold as a slave to a high official named Potiphar, and God began to bless him. We read, "The LORD was with him and…the LORD caused all that he did to prosper in his hand" (Genesis 39:3). Because of this, Joseph began to receive favor from his overseer, which was wonderful—until he also caught the attention of Potiphar's wife. "Joseph was handsome in form and appearance" (verse 6), so she also thought of a few things for Joseph to do—things that involved her.

Joseph could not comply with her requests or sexual advances because he refused to sin against his master or his God. Hell hath no fury like a woman scorned, and Potiphar's wife was no exception. She quickly accused Joseph of rape and had him imprisoned.

Being imprisoned for doing good must have been a very bitter experience for Joseph. He went to jail on a lie. It's bad enough that his family messed him over, but to do an excellent job only to be lied about, sent to prison, and deprived of everything he had worked to attain…these could have put a bitter taste in Joseph's mouth.

Yet even in jail, "The LORD was with Joseph and extended kindness to him, and gave him favor" (Genesis 39:21). Because of this, Joseph was promoted to a position of responsibility in the jail. Joseph didn't sit, sulk, and sour. Rather, he got busy doing the best he could with what he had where he was.

When things get bitter, we shouldn't ask, "Why am I going through this?" Rather, we should ask, "Lord, how do You want to use this to help me fulfill my destiny?" When you don't ask the right question, you will get frustrated. You will spend your time dwelling on issues of fairness rather than looking to see what God is going to do.

Joseph didn't dwell on the bitter. Rather, he acted responsibly on the assignment he had been given. After he had spent some time in the prison, a couple of his fellow inmates had dreams. God empowered Joseph to interpret the dreams, and he told his friends the meaning of what they had seen. One man, who had been the king's cupbearer, had dreamed of being released and reinstated, and Joseph asked him to remember him when that happened.

> "Lord, how do You want to use this to help me fulfill my destiny?"

"Yet the chief cupbearer did not remember Joseph, but forgot him" (Genesis 40:23). Just when Joseph thought he might see a change coming, his situation grew even more bitter. The chief cupbearer was set free. He was reinstated to his position, just as Joseph had said he would be. Yet he also forgot all about Joseph—that is, until Pharaoh also had a dream that he couldn't interpret.

Finally the cupbearer remembered Joseph and called on him to interpret Pharaoh's dream. Pharaoh was clearly impressed.

> Since God has informed you of all this, there is no one so discerning and wise as you are. You shall be over my house, and according to your command all my people shall do homage; only in the throne I will be greater than you (Genesis 41:39-40).

Joseph was suddenly thrust from behind bars straight to the boardroom. And finally, God fulfilled the dream He had given Joseph and positioned him in a place of power over his family. The same brothers who had once betrayed him, selling him into slavery, later knelt before him (though they didn't recognize him), asking for food during a famine. Through a series of events, Joseph's brothers ended up alone with him, and he decided to reveal himself to them. He sent everyone else out, pulled his brothers near to him, and showed them that he was truly their brother Joseph. By then, Joseph looked and spoke like an Egyptian. Yet Joseph still carried the mark of a Hebrew. He was circumcised. Revealing himself to his brothers, Joseph attempted to comfort them with his wisdom. "Do not be grieved or angry with yourselves, because you sold me here, for God sent me before you to preserve life" (Genesis 45:5).

A few chapters later, Joseph delivered the Bible's greatest statement on destiny: "As for you, you meant evil against me, but God meant it for good in order to bring about this present result" (Genesis 50:20). The bitter scenario that others intended for Joseph and that Joseph endured unfairly was transformed into good when God brought about His perfect purpose.

Friend, if you've had bitter experiences—things that have the potential to make you bitter—they do not have the final say. They are not the defining factors in who you are. If your parents, your spouse, or your employer didn't treat you right; if you struggle with infirmity, addictions, or emotional insecurities...none of that defines your destiny.

Sometimes people treat you wrong, and as they walk away, they claim you will never be able to make it on your own. They fill your head with lies of defeat—but they are *lies*. These people may have deserted you, yet their exodus only opened the door for the right kind of people to enter your life. If people are putting negative thoughts into your mind and spirit about you, they are not a part of the destiny God has for you. Yes, God may use them to humble you, strengthen you, and move you along the path toward your purpose. But rather than hang on to negative relationships that wear you down, let them go. You are a product of your past, not a prisoner. Let it go. Let them go.

> Bitter experiences don't define your destiny.

Just as God reunited Joseph and his brothers, God may bring people back into your life when they are ready to relate to you in a productive, healthy manner. But until then, let them go. Don't allow bitter events or bitter people to keep you from achieving and optimizing your destiny in every way. I know it hurts when people turn against you. But remember Joseph's words: "As for you, you meant evil against me, but God meant it for good in order to bring about this present result." Let it go. Let the bitterness go. God allowed those negative people and those negative circumstances to make you who you are today. Just as He had a plan for Joseph, He has a plan to use all of the bitter events in your life for good. Somewhere down the line, He will work through you to help someone else who has been hurt, abandoned, lied about, broken... someone who is looking for hope.

View your pain theologically, not socially. Don't just say, "That's not fair." Rather, say, "God, even though that's not fair, I believe You are going to use it so I can fulfill my destiny. I trust You to use the bitter things in my life for Your glory."

You're right, it's not fair. That thing that happened to you that you had no control over—it's not fair. But God is a master at turning unfair things into miracles when we let Him. Choose not to block His work in your life by harboring bitterness, anger, and hate. Tell Him it wasn't fair, and then tell Him you are going to let it go, sit back, and watch Him use it for good. God is a just God. Let Him have it. He will bring about justice if you step out of the way and let Him. Trust Him with the deepest, most authentic faith within you.

God can make the bitter things in your life better. He can make the good things great. He can cover the bad with His grace. In the next chapter, we'll see how the good, the bad, and the bitter can intersect and lead to your destiny.

Intersections

10

You have an assignment to fulfill. You have a destiny. We've looked at the way your destiny relates to your passion, vision, gifts, and experiences. Now I want to discuss how all of these connect in what I call a *divine intersection*.

An intersection is a place where things converge. When you reach an intersection while driving, cars coming from one direction converge with cars coming from another direction. They intersect.

One way for you to discover your destiny is to watch the pieces of your life intersecting in a divinely ordained way.

Chasing Donkeys

First Samuel contains one of the greatest biblical illustrations of a divine intersection. We read about Saul, who would later be chosen as the first king of Israel, going about his normal business of taking care of his father's donkeys. One day, some of the donkeys got lost.

> Now the donkeys of Kish, Saul's father, were lost. So Kish said to his son Saul, "Take now with you one of the servants, and arise, go search for the donkeys." He passed through the hill country of Ephraim and passed through the land of Shalishah, but they did not find them. Then they passed through the land of Shaalim, but they were not

there. Then he passed through the land of the Benjamites, but they did not find them (1 Samuel 9:3-4).

In Saul's day, donkeys were used to carry things. Donkeys were about as common as vehicles are today. So when Saul's father's donkeys went missing, Saul set about to track them down. He wasn't doing anything special or unusual. Saul was merely going about his regular routine. However, this time he couldn't find the donkeys. Saul searched in several locations but came up empty.

After Saul had spent enough time searching for the donkeys, he adopted a quitter's mentality. "When they came to the land of Zuph, Saul said to his servant who was with him, 'Come, and let us return, or else my father will cease to be concerned about the donkeys and will become anxious for us'" (verse 5). In other words, Saul said, "The game is up. The search is over. Let's call it quits and go home."

Saul wasn't about to spend any more time on a mundane task that appeared endless. Because of his frustration and hopelessness, he wanted to throw in the towel. But right at that time, Saul's servant advised him to keep going. He suggested they seek out a man of God who might be able to help them.

Why talk with a spiritual man (a prophet) about a natural problem (lost donkeys)? Saul's servant had deftly moved from Saul's earthly frustration to a heavenly realization. He connected the routine activity to the spiritual realm. He brought heaven to bear on earth in order to hear from God about the ordinary, which is critical for discovering the divine intersections in life.

> We begin discovering our divine intersections when we seek God in the midst of our normal, everyday events.

Some of us have such an ethereal view of God, He exists only outside of the realm of sight and sound. But God is intricately involved in the everyday activities of life (Deuteronomy 4:7; Matthew 10:29-30). We begin discovering our divine intersections when we seek God in the midst of our normal, everyday events. When we keep our eyes open to the spiritual, we will see the spiritual. But if we keep our eyes focused on the natural, we will miss out on the spiritual.

As Saul and his servant were chasing donkeys, the servant gave Saul golden advice. He told him to seek the prophet, who in this case was Samuel.

Connecting at the Intersection

As you carry out your normal routine, God sets up situations and intersections for you to enter. As He prepares you for the destiny and future He has for you, He also prepares others for you. He creates the perfect scenario for situations and people in your life to connect at just the right time, leading you to fulfill your destiny.

You may think that you are in a dead-end career right now. Or perhaps you see no end to changing diapers, washing clothes, and chauffeuring your children around to their different events. Perhaps you've had a dream in your heart—a passion—for quite some time, and yet you see no real connection between that dream and your current daily activities. If you feel that way, remember Saul and his donkeys. As Saul was wandering about the countryside doing nothing more significant than fixing a flat tire, getting his oil changed, or looking for some transportation, God was busy hooking up Saul's intersection. He was speaking to the prophet whom Saul's servant would lead him to.

> Now a day before Saul's coming, the LORD had revealed this to Samuel saying, "About this time tomorrow I will send you a man from the land of Benjamin, and you shall anoint him to be prince over My people Israel; and he will deliver My people from the hand of the Philistines" (1 Samuel 9:15-16).

Did you catch the connection? Saul is not out looking for a kingship—he's looking for donkeys. Yet God tells Samuel that He has a purpose and a plan for this man. He tells Samuel to get ready because He is about to make a divine connection at an earthly intersection.

In fact, we see God arranging a three-way connection. At the end of verse 16, we read, "I have regarded My people, because their cry has come to Me." In one direction we see Saul out chasing donkeys. In another direction we see Samuel looking for a man to anoint. In yet another direction the people of God are crying out for a leader. God intercepts each party at just the right time to make their paths intersect.

But keep in mind that Saul will find Samuel only if he listens to his servant and doesn't quit. Saul wanted to throw in the towel, but someone in his life was willing to nudge him and point him in the right direction. Like Saul, you absolutely must have people in your life who won't let you quit. Sometimes life really does make you want to throw up your hands and cry uncle. It's tough. It's long. You don't see your change on the horizon. If you are on the path to God's purpose for you, you need someone to encourage you to keep going, keep pressing, and keep hoping.

> You absolutely must have people in your life who won't let you quit.

That someone may be a friend. It could be your pastor, a preacher on the television or radio, an article you read, a Facebook or Twitter post, or a book. Make sure to position yourself where you can be encouraged because you will encounter resistance along the path to your destiny. You will face difficulties as you chase your own donkeys. Boredom may tempt you to give up as well. Unless you learn to connect the physical with the spiritual, the ordinary with the extraordinary, you will miss your anointing. The donkeys of life are tools in the hand of the Master. They can lead you straight to your destiny.

Saul is not out and about trying to find his destiny. He's out trying to find his donkeys. Yet while he's trying to find his donkeys, he will discover his destiny. When he attaches God to his ordinary (with his servant's help), the result will be extraordinary. Not only that, but it will put him in a position to help others. Keep in mind that your divine intersections in life are not only about you. They will always somehow benefit God's people and promote God's kingdom.

Saul's divine intersection came as a result of God hearing the cries of His people. Saul was the answer God was raising up for them. God's purposes are always attached to His kingdom perspective. In fact, you just may be the answer to someone else's prayer if you make yourself available to seek God and His kingdom rather than simply keep your eyes on the donkeys.

The Word of God to You

When Samuel saw Saul the next day, God revealed to him that Saul was the man He had spoken about. So Samuel invited Saul to dinner and told him he would have a message for him the next morning. Following a night of dinner, Samuel told Saul to send his servant on ahead of them because he wanted to give Saul a word from God. Saul had come to the prophet looking for his donkeys, but he was about to leave with something much bigger than that because God had a word just for him. God's word is always greater than what you are looking for. His purpose for you is a lot larger than what you have envisioned. Not only that, God's word is personal.

Samuel said, "Say to the servant that he might go ahead of us and pass on, but you remain standing now, that I may proclaim the word of God *to you*" (1 Samuel 9:27). I want to be sure you caught the distinction. The words "to you" are very important because the

> God's purpose for you is a lot larger than what you have envisioned.

word of God *to you* is very different from the Word of God. The New Testament refers to the *logos*, which we understand often refers to the inscribed, written Scripture. Another Greek term for *word, rhema*, often refers to the spoken word of God, or the word of God *to you*. God sometimes highlights a passage on your soul, as when you hear a sermon preached that has your name written all over it.

Sometimes people read their Bibles and say, "I was blessed by that passage," or they come to church and say, "I was touched by today's message." But this is different from someone saying, "God told me exactly what I need to do through this passage [or sermon]." That is why God's Word says, "Do not despise prophetic utterances" (1 Thessalonians 5:20). Do not reject God's word to you.

Of course you need to test the spirit behind the utterance because God's *rhema* will never contradict His *logos*. People may say, "Jesus told me to tell you such and such," but that doesn't guarantee they have a prophetic word. Their proclamation must line up with Scripture. In addition, God will often confirm it through circumstances or situations as well, just as He did in the case of Saul. To go from chasing donkeys to ruling a nation is no small change. Samuel didn't expect Saul to simply take his word for it. He predicted a series of circumstances that would confirm to Saul's heart and soul that what Samuel had spoken was true. Sometimes we call these signs or confirmations. They are situations that God allows to validate His *rhema*. In Saul's case, there were many.

> Then Samuel took the flask of oil, poured it on his head, kissed him and said, "Has not the LORD anointed you a ruler over His inheritance? When you go from me today, then you will find two men close to Rachel's tomb in the territory of Benjamin at Zelzah; and they will say to you, 'The donkeys which you went to look for have been found. Now behold, your father has ceased to be concerned about the donkeys and is anxious for you, saying, "What shall I do about my son?"' Then you will go on further from there, and you will come as far as the oak of Tabor, and there three men going up to God at Bethel will meet you, one carrying three young goats, another carrying three loaves of bread, and another carrying a jug of wine; and they will greet you and give you two loaves of bread, which you will accept from their hand. Afterward you will come to the hill of God where the Philistine garrison is; and it shall be as soon as you have come there to the city, that you will meet a group of prophets coming down from the high place with harp, tambourine, flute, and a lyre before them, and they will be prophesying. Then the Spirit of the LORD will come upon you mightily, and you shall prophesy with

them and be *changed into another man*. It shall be when these signs come to you, do for yourself what the occasion requires, *for God is with you*" (1 Samuel 10:1-7).

Samuel said that his word from God to Saul would be confirmed through a series of events. God confirmed externally to Saul what He communicated internally to Samuel. Frequently, God will validate what He says with a sign. Now, keep in mind that Scripture tells us that "the heart is more deceitful than all else" (Jeremiah 17:9). You can trick yourself if you look for a sign in everything.

The first thing you must always do is confirm that the *rhema* spoken to you or highlighted through Scripture is backed by God's Word—be certain that it doesn't contradict the truth God has already revealed. Next, when you feel that God has given a word to you, ask Him to provide a divine confirmation. If you are looking for a mate, don't just ask God to give you a sign that the next single man or single woman you come across will be your husband or wife. No, ask for something that reflects the divine.

When Gideon heard a word from God to him, he wanted to be sure, so he put out a fleece and asked God to make the ground dry but to keep the fleece wet with dew. When that happened, Gideon still wanted to be extra sure, so he asked God to do what seemed even more impossible—to make the fleece dry while the ground all around it was wet with dew. The word that had been spoken to Gideon was confirmed by a divine sign, just as the word that was spoken to Saul was confirmed through multiple divine signs.

Merging the Natural with the Divine

When God leads you from where you are to a divine intersection, your gifts, skills, passion, experience, and purpose will merge. He will have prepared you for that experience, and He will have prepared that experience for you. First Samuel tells us that "God changed his heart" (1 Samuel 10:9), and Saul became a new man. When you step into your anointing, you will receive the Spirit's power to carry out His plan. There will be a certain flow about what you do—it will feel natural to you in many ways. In sports, we refer to this as being in the zone. As a believer, you enter the zone when God orchestrates your intersection—when all things merge. Saul met his purpose while he was out chasing donkeys. You never know what God will use to usher you into your destiny.

Friend, if you learn anything at all from Saul, learn this: Don't go searching for your destiny. Go searching for your donkeys. In other words, fulfill your routine responsibilities and attach those routine responsibilities to God. When you include God in your routine, the natural becomes supernatural. You discover your destiny when the natural merges with the divine.

> You discover your destiny when the natural merges with the divine.

Don't worry about locating your destiny if you are seeking after God because your destiny will locate you. You will discover it in the divine intersection that God has planned for you. Moses's intersection with Pharaoh's daughter on the Nile positioned him to eventually set God's people free.

When Queen Esther's husband couldn't sleep and asked for something to read, he was brought the book of history, and he heard the account of Mordecai saving him. This eventually led to the Israelites' empowerment to defend themselves against their enemies and escape certain death. Mordecai's experiences, the book of history, the king who was unable to sleep, and Haman's desire to annihilate the Jews all merged at a divine intersection.

Time after time the Bible gives us illustrations of divine intersections. Abigail offered David's army some food just in time to stop a rampage on her home. Abigail's foolish husband later died, and she became the king's wife. Ruth gleaned in Boaz's field, and she eventually became a matriarch in the line of Jesus Christ.

You never know how God is going to bring things together at just the right time. Intersections are happening all around you, but you need to open your eyes in order to see them. You probably won't see if, like Saul, you don't attach the supernatural to the natural. You need to ask, "Why does God have me out here searching for these donkeys for so long?" Resist the temptation to complain or give up altogether. In order to see and experience the intersections in your life that God has for you, view life through the lens of your spirit. Don't just use your eyes.

By the way, Saul eventually got his donkeys back after all. Even though his search was about much more than locating his donkeys, God gave him the donkeys as well. So keep searching, keep trying, keep looking, and keep doing that which God has you doing right now, even if it seems to have no possible connection to your destiny. If this is what God has given you to do right now, then do it with all of your heart. Keep chasing your donkeys while connecting heaven's view with earth, and eventually you will come to a divine intersection that involves your future.

PART 3

The Imperatives
of Your Destiny

Commitment   11

I love sports. I played just about every sport our school offered. In the fall I played football, and during the winter I swam on the swim team. In the spring I played baseball. And every weekend, regardless of the season, you could find me playing tackle football without any pads with anyone who showed up.

On the football team, I was the quarterback. On the baseball team, I was the catcher. Many people may not know about one unique strategy catchers employ. They not only give the signals to the pitcher but also try to disrupt the batter. Every good catcher knows how to mess with the batter's head. You say whatever you can—or don't say anything at all—to take the batter off his game. Where I come from, we call that "talking noise." It includes anything that distracts the batter from doing what he came to do.

Yogi Berra was one of the most noted catchers of all time. One day, Yogi, who played for the New York Yankees, was taunting an equally legendary player, Hank Aaron, who was playing for the Milwaukee Braves. When Hank came up to bat, Yogi started in, trying to distract him. He said Hank would hit better if he would hold the bat right. "You're supposed to hit with the label up on the bat," Yogi said. Hank turned and said, "I came up here to hit, not to read."[3]

Friend, you have to know why you are here. If you don't, other people can throw you off. If you don't know your purpose, the circumstances around you can distract you. In fact, any old jostle may cause you to miss the ball because you will be unfocused and off balance. As a result, you will end up striking out and wasting your opportunity at bat.

Redeem the Time

The book of Ecclesiastes tells us, "There is an appointed time for everything. And there is a time for every event under heaven" (Ecclesiastes 3:1). It also says God "has made everything appropriate in its time" (verse 11).

God has a clock. Yet God Himself is not obligated to the clock because He is eternal. God sits outside of the clock. However, you and I are obligated to the clock because we are still bound by time. That's why Paul tells us in his letter to the church at Ephesus, "Be careful how you walk, not as unwise men but as wise, *making the most of your time*, because the days are evil. So then do not be foolish, but understand what the will of the Lord is" (Ephesians 5:15-16).

The King James and New King James versions say we are to be "redeeming the time." Make the most of it, don't waste it, and definitely don't squander it by not understanding God's purpose for your time.

> Time has been given to you for one reason—so you can fulfill your destiny.

Time has been given to you for one reason—so you can fulfill your destiny. If you are still alive and you still have time, that time has been given to you in order to achieve the destiny God has ordained for you.

Time is consistent with destiny and purpose.

When you have to get up and go to work in the morning, you will set your clock to six a.m. or whatever time you choose that will get you to your destination on schedule. This is because time is tied to purpose. If you don't live on purpose, you will not use your time wisely. You will get up anytime you feel like it, go to bed anytime, and let the days slip by without redeeming the time. And before you know it, you are 50, 60, or 70 years old, and you wonder, "Where did all the time go?"

Your time and the way you use it are intimately linked with your purpose and destiny. Knowing and living out your purpose gives you God's perspective on the use of your time.

Now, you might be thinking, "Tony, I got saved when I was twenty, but I didn't get serious about my purpose until now—some thirty years later. What now? I have already wasted too much time."

If that is you, then I want you to focus right now on God's grace because Scripture tells us that God can give you back the time you have lost. He says, "I will make up to you for the years that the swarming locust has eaten" (Joel 2:25). God will not go back in time and make you 20 years old again, but He has a way of pouring a lot of purpose into the years you have left.

> He has a way of pouring a lot of purpose into the years you have left.

In addition, I want to encourage you to do your part. Maybe you just strolled through the first decades of your adult life, and now you realize that time is running short. If that is you, then picture yourself in a sprint to the finish line. Don't keep strolling. Don't view this as a marathon. Sprint to the end. Maximize your time now. Do as much now to fulfill your destiny as you possibly can—and then some. Make the most of your remaining time.

A Living Sacrifice

As we have seen earlier, your destiny is the customized life calling God has ordained and equipped you to accomplish in order to bring Him the greatest glory and achieve the maximum expansion of His kingdom. Your destiny explains why you are here. What a tragedy it would be to die without knowing why God saved you in the first place, to have only meandered from place to place, thing to thing, or person to person without fulfilling your destiny.

Your commitment to God is the starting point for discovering and living out your destiny.

> I urge you, brethren, by the mercies of God, to present your bodies a living and holy sacrifice, acceptable to God, which is your spiritual service of worship. And do not be conformed to this world, but be transformed by the renewing of your mind, *so that you may prove what the will of God is,* that which is good and acceptable and perfect (Romans 12:1-2).

As we see in this passage, when you are positioned rightly underneath God, you won't have to find your destiny because your destiny will find you. The leading of the Holy Spirit, the will of God, and your destiny are all directly connected. But in order to be positioned rightly and to be led by the Spirit into the will of God, you must first allow God to own all of you. You are to present your body a living and holy sacrifice, acceptable to God.

You must first allow God to own all of you.

The phrase "living and holy sacrifice" conveys an interesting concept. It is somewhat contradictory because Old Testament sacrifices were killed. If a lamb was sacrificed, it was put on the altar and slain. Therefore, it was dead. Essentially, then, in order to present yourself as a living sacrifice, you are offering to God something that is both alive and dead—all at the same time.

If Paul were here with us today, he would probably quote himself: "I have been crucified with Christ; and it is no longer I who live, but Christ lives in me" (Galatians 2:20). Paul was alive—he was writing or dictating those words—but he was also crucified, or dead.

Imagine asking Paul, "Hey Paul, what are your dreams? What are your goals?" He might reply, "I don't have any dreams or goals because dead folks don't dream. Dead folks don't have goals."

But suppose you switched the questions a bit and asked, "Paul, what is God's dream for you? What are His goals for your life?" Then Paul would be able to talk in depth because he defined his life not in terms of his own will but in terms of his identity with Jesus Christ. As he wrote, "You have been bought with a price: therefore glorify God in your body" (1 Corinthians 6:20).

Paul's career was not the sum total of his destiny, as a matter of fact. Paul made God's goals his own goals, so he was able to carry out the seemingly mundane career of making tents in order to earn the money he needed to carry out his destiny—to make God known. When you know your life belongs to Christ, you can be content in any career or occupation God has you in as long as you know it is enabling you to live out your destiny and benefit others.

God is not primarily interested in blessing your destiny for your own sake. He is primarily interested in blessing your destiny for His sake. The best way to live with that mindset is to offer yourself to Him as a living sacrifice, to climb up on the altar and stay there. The problem is, most of us will respond to a good sermon, song, or quiet time with God and climb right up onto the altar, saying, "Not my will, but yours." But then we are just as quick to climb back down off the altar the next day. That's the trouble with living sacrifices.

One day a chicken and a pig walked past a grocery store. A sign in the store window read, Needed: Bacon and Eggs. The chicken looked at the pig, and the pig looked at the chicken. The chicken said, "I'll give him the eggs if you give him the bacon."

"You have to be crazy," said the pig. "Have you lost your mind?"

"What's the problem?" asked the chicken.

The pig replied, "The problem is that for you it is a contribution. But for me, it's my life!"

A lot of people today want to give God a contribution. They will give an egg here or there—or maybe even a dozen from time to time. But they don't want to climb up on the altar and die to their own wants, desires, dreams, and will so they can be maximized for God's purpose as living sacrifices. But God doesn't want your eggs. He wants your pork chops, ham hocks, and pig's feet. He wants the whole deal.

Motivated by Mercy

Before Paul asserted in Romans 12 that we are to be living sacrifices, he wrote in Romans 1–11 about the mercies of God. What is the difference between grace and mercy? In God's grace, He gives us what we don't deserve. In God's mercy, He doesn't give us what we do deserve— He withholds the punishment that is due us.

In Romans 1–3, Paul explains that all those who have rejected God are condemned. He offers three groups as examples. Heathens are condemned because they rejected God even though He revealed Himself in nature and in their consciences. Jews are condemned because they rejected God in spite of the oracles predicting Christ. Moralists are condemned because they condemn others for that which they practice themselves. Paul summarizes by saying that no one falls outside of the legitimate condemnation of God. "As it is written, 'There is none righteous, not even one'" (Romans 3:10).

Paul follows up his writing on mankind's guilt before God by telling us that God has come up with a way for unrighteous people to be made righteous. In this process, called *justification*, God credits the righteousness of Christ to the account of the unrighteous. Chapter 4 tells how we are to receive this righteousness by faith, and chapter 5 shows that once you are endowed by grace, it ought to affect all of your life.

However, chapters 6 and 7 explain that even though grace ought to affect all of your life, it doesn't always do so. The effectiveness of grace in your life depends on whom you obey—yourself or God. Chapter 8 shows how a believer can have victory to obey God through the Holy Spirit, whose job is to empower those whom God has saved so they can live out their salvation. But then chapters 9–11 go on to explain that people do not receive that power if they do not believe it.

Through all of this, Paul has made a clear argument that we can receive God's great mercies if we will believe. Then he says, "Therefore I urge you, brethren, by the mercies of God..." Paul is asking us to recognize our own unrighteousness, our own inability to live holy lives, our own incapacity to save ourselves...and then to present ourselves to God as living and holy sacrifices in response to His mercy on us.

All of You and All of God

Friend, your destiny includes your total commitment to God. Church attendance without total commitment becomes sacrilege rather than worship. As you embark on the journey of destiny, this is one of the deepest questions you need to ask yourself: Does all of me belong to all of Him? Or do you have a spiritual attic in your life—a place where you put stuff you don't want God to touch? Commitment requires that *all of you* belongs to *all of God*.

In order for all of you to belong to all of God, the world must own none of you. We have seen that Paul emphasized this point: "Do not be conformed to this world, but be transformed by the renewing of your mind." Being conformed to something is similar to what happens when a potter molds a lump of clay. The potter squeezes, shapes, and forms the clay until it conforms to what the potter had intended.

> Your destiny includes your total commitment to God.

Paul is telling us that we are not to allow the world's way of thinking or the world's way of operating to conform us to the world's standards. The world system is headed by Satan and leaves God out. Many people have not discovered their destiny because they are letting the world define success for them. When that happens, you may have wealth and all that money can buy, but you won't have your destiny and the joy, peace, and contentment that accompany it.

If you are to reach your destiny, you cannot let the world own you. You must belong to God. When you belong to God, you will be "transformed by the renewing of your mind." The Greek word translated *transformed* is in the passive tense. This means that the transformation is not something you do for yourself; God does it for you. If I were to tell you that I drove to the store, I would be using an active construction to describe something I did. However, if I told you that I was driven to the store, I would be using a passive construction to explain that someone else did something to me or for me.

138 DISCOVER YOUR DESTINY

A Clear Mind

In other words, when you commit your life to God and give Him all of you, not allowing the world to have anything of you, you have positioned yourself so the Holy Spirit can go to work in your mind. He will do the work if you will position yourself rightly underneath God as a living and holy sacrifice. Rather than being double-minded, as James says, or rather than living in spiritual schizophrenia, you will have a clear mind because of the Spirit's work within you. As the Spirit begins to work in your mind, transforming it, He will reveal the will of God to you. "For as he thinks within himself, so he is" (Proverbs 23:7). The way to have your thoughts align with God's thoughts is to commit yourself to Him. You align yourself underneath His will, presenting yourself as a living sacrifice to Him and rejecting worldly thoughts.

> The way to have your thoughts align with God's thoughts is to commit yourself to Him.

When the Holy Spirit transforms your mind, He replaces your old, worldly way of thinking with His thoughts. You are then thinking the thoughts of the Trinity—God the Father, Jesus Christ His Son, and the Holy Spirit.

Therefore, you can then boldly practice John 15:7-8: "If you abide in Me, and My words abide in you, ask whatever you wish, and it will be done for you. My Father is glorified by this, that you bear much fruit, and so prove to be My disciples." You can now get on your knees and pray for whatever you are thinking because your mind is conformed to Christ. You are wanting and desiring what He wants.

Get in Position

Fulfilling your destiny is all about aligning yourself under God, positioning yourself rightly under His leadership. A great quarterback can hit a receiver even when defensive backs are rushing as long as his receiver is in the right position. In fact, football coaches don't merely look for speed when recruiting receivers. Football coaches look for the way receivers position themselves. Michael Irvin of the Dallas Cowboys was not the fastest receiver on the field, but he could get positioned correctly, creating a target that his quarterback could hit. God can hit you with your destiny if you are in position.

If you are an experienced sailor, you understand that trying to get the wind to change directions is not the best idea. You might be out there a long time if that is your strategy. Rather, you have to adjust your sail to the direction of the wind in order to make any headway. God wants to give you your destiny, but you must adjust your sails according to the direction He is blowing in order to get you where He wants you to go.

> God can hit you with your destiny if you are in position.

A Perfect Destiny

There is no greater destiny for you than the destiny God has for you. It is the best plan for you. Live it. God's destiny for you is "good and acceptable and perfect." You don't need to be afraid that if you commit all of you to all of God, He will give you a destiny that you hate. God will use your personality, talents, backgrounds, skills, interests, passion, and even your scars to bring you to a destiny that is "good and acceptable and perfect." Not too many people wind up hating a perfect destiny.

According to my thoughts and according to my plans, I was never supposed to be in Dallas, where I've been pastoring now for more than 36 years. I had made plans straight out of college to go Grace Theological Seminary in Indiana. I had applied, been accepted, paid my fees, found housing, and prepared to move when God showed up through a conversation with a man who said, "Tony, have you ever thought of going to Dallas Theological Seminary? I'll pay your application fee if you will commit to pray about it and apply."

Which I did. And that placed me in an urban context while studying for both my master's degree and my doctorate. Grace Theological would not have provided an urban context of ministry at all. Going to Dallas opened the door to an entire urban-focused outreach ministry that now takes place both locally and nationally in an effort to connect churches with schools to impact struggling communities through the National Church Adopt-a-School Initiative.

From a human standpoint, most people would say I changed my mind. Yet according to Romans 12:1-2, the Holy Spirit transformed my thinking. He caused me to think differently because He had a plan for me.

A little girl came to her father one day and said, "Daddy, you promised to give me a nickel." Her father had promised her. So he reached in his pocket, but he couldn't find a nickel. Instead, all he had were dollar bills. In fact, the smallest bill he had was a $20.

He said, "You've been a really good girl lately, so here is a twenty-dollar bill instead."

The little girl started to cry. "But Daddy," she said, "you promised me a nickel."

"But sweetie," he replied, "this is a whole bunch of nickels."

Yet because she could not understand, tears streamed down her face.

This is what a lot of us do with our destiny. We tell God what we want to do with our lives. We tell Him what we desire. But God says that if you will simply commit all of you to all of Him, He has so much more to give you than just what you want. God wants you to take the risk of trusting Him. He wants to hear you say, "Not my will, but Your will be done." Even if God's purpose includes a cross on Friday, remember—there will be a resurrection on Sunday. Trust Him. He has a good, acceptable, and perfect destiny just for you.

Development 12

The book of Exodus contains one of the greatest biblical stories related to destiny. Most of us are familiar with Moses. We know how he floated in a basket along the Nile until Pharaoh's daughter found him. We know about the ten plagues and the parting of the Red Sea. We know that he led the Israelites out of bondage and into freedom.

However, we can easily miss the significance of what happened during a period of Moses's life that the Bible has very little to say about. Not much is written concerning the time between Moses's fortieth year (when he fled from Egypt) until his eightieth year (when he met God at the burning bush). Even though there isn't much written about those four decades, they are critical. During those years, Moses developed the way he needed to in order to fulfill his destiny.

A Valley of Development

The road to your destiny passes through a valley of development. This is where God prepares you for your destiny and prepares everything and everyone else related to your destiny for you.

Most of us don't like to think about going through a time of development. It doesn't usually make for the greatest stories in the Bible either. When we consider Moses, we recall things like the Red Sea or the burning bush. But Moses's destiny didn't begin there. It began much earlier than either of those situations. It started in a time of preparation. It began during many long and drawn-out days when Moses took care of things that did not seem all too spectacular. He shepherded sheep each day and ate his meal by a fire each night. His preparation began in trials, challenges, and boredom.

And just as God had a plan for Moses, He also has a plan to prepare you and lead you to your destiny. A developmental process must occur so that when you arrive at your bush, you are ready for your calling, and just as importantly, your calling and all that it entails are ready for you.

> God has a plan to prepare you and lead you to your destiny.

Before Moses saw a bush on fire, and before he led the Israelites out of slavery, God allowed and arranged a series of events that helped him develop. In the New Testament, Stephen summarizes Moses's life in Acts 7—the last sermon he preaches before he is martyred. Stephen spends a significant amount of time recounting the history of the Jewish nation, which obviously included a portion on Moses. For the sake of our discussion on undergoing development to fulfill your destiny, we need to look at Moses's entire story, or what might be called the backstory. In it we discover how God prepared him for his destiny.

It was at this time that Moses was born; and he was lovely in the sight of God, and he was nurtured three months in his father's home. And after he had been set outside, Pharaoh's daughter took him away and nurtured him as her own son. Moses was educated in all the learning of the Egyptians, and he was a man of power in words and deeds. But when he was approaching the age of forty, it entered his mind to visit his brethren, the sons of Israel. And when he saw one of them being treated unjustly, he defended him and took vengeance for the oppressed by striking down the Egyptian. And he supposed that his brethren understood that

God was granting them deliverance through him, but they did not understand. On the following day he appeared to them as they were fighting together, and he tried to reconcile them in peace, saying "Men, you are brethren, why do you injure one another?" But the one who was injuring his neighbor pushed him away, saying, "Who made you a ruler and judge over us? You do not mean to kill me as you killed the Egyptian yesterday, do you?" At this remark, Moses fled and became an alien in the land of Midian, where he became the father of two sons (Acts 7:20-29).

This overview of Moses's life provides us with a few key points. Moses was raised in Pharaoh's household, so he would have experienced the finer, more luxurious things of life. He would also have received the best education Egypt had to offer. At that time, Egypt was the most advanced nation in the world—they had built the pyramids and had developed systems of writing. The best education in Egypt would have been the best education in the world. For his day and for his culture, Moses was brilliant. We are also told that Moses was mighty in the way he spoke and in the things he did. He was an attractive, intelligent, privileged, powerful, and skilled man—the cream of the crop. Everyone knew Moses. More than likely, everyone wanted to be him too.

In addition to being exposed to everything Egypt had to offer, Moses was exposed to Hebrew culture and values through his biological mother. As we have seen, when Moses was taken from the river and raised in Pharaoh's home, his sister Miriam asked Pharaoh's daughter if she would like a nursemaid to help care for him. That nursemaid turned out to be Moses's own mother, who was then able to raise her son in the protection of the Egyptian palace.

So Moses benefited from the best of Egypt and received instruction and wisdom from his Hebrew mother along the way. At 40, Moses was at the top of his game in every way. He had position and power, and he had a sense of his destiny. He knew the plight of his brothers, the Hebrews, and he decided to set them free, apparently one person at a time.

Backfire

We read in Hebrews that Moses made a decision to identify with the Jews rather than the Egyptians (Hebrews 11:24-26), which led to his belief that he would deliver Israel all by himself. Moses had a vague understanding of his purpose—he just wasn't ready to fulfill it. He had not developed into the person God could use.

Moses's plan had a few flaws. First, God hadn't specifically instructed him to deliver Israel, so God didn't provide the power Moses would have needed to pull off the job. Second, the Israelites didn't know what Moses was trying to do, so they couldn't grasp why he killed the Egyptian. The passage says, "They did not understand" (Acts 7:25).

Friend, God will reveal your destiny when He is ready for you to receive it. The passion might be in you, the skills might be in you, and the burden, desire, and dream might all be in you. But until God says go, you are not ready to fulfill it. When Moses killed the Egyptian, he acted on his burden, passion, and skills. He even appeared to be at an intersection of sorts. But he acted in his flesh rather than waiting on God to reveal his steps. As a result, Moses's move backfired in epic proportions.

> God will reveal your destiny when He is ready for you to receive it.

Moses assumed that he had the right time, he had the right method, and he was the right man. Yet only one of his assumptions was right. He was the right man, but his timing, methodology, and everything else were all wrong. God hadn't yet developed Moses to the point where he could lead an entire nation to its freedom. And because Moses jumped out ahead of his destiny, he ended up making a very wrong move. As a result, he fled to the wilderness, winding up at Midian, where he met Jethro, married his daughter, and herded sheep.

For 40 years.

Moses went from the White House to the outhouse and worked long hours for low pay in the hot sun taking care of sheep.

Humility

At the height of Moses's development, he learned a lesson of humility. Most of us need to learn this lesson sometime. It is a lesson of inadequacy. God will often use valleys and hardships to strip us of self-sufficiency because self-sufficiency negates dependence on Him.

Moses had his burden. He knew his passion. He had skills, money, looks, power, position, intelligence, and strength. He just didn't know what each

> There is only one God, and we are not Him.

of us needs to know most—that there is only one God, and we are not Him. Moses thought more of himself than he should have.

So God took Moses to the wilderness to learn what he never could in Egypt. He took him to a place of nothing. He took him to a dead-end career. He took Moses to a foreign land where he had to unlearn one culture and learn another. He had to pick up a new language and a new lifestyle. He learned how to lead sheep—a skill that would come in handy when he eventually led people through the wilderness. God took away the things Moses could fall back on. His Egyptian education had no real value out there in the wilderness. Moses needed to learn how to survive in the wilderness. How to find water. How to protect sheep. How to make his own sandals and his own staff.

Essentially, Moses had to unlearn much of what he had learned in order to learn what he needed to know most—that he didn't know nearly as much as he thought he did in the first place.

The Time Has Come

We discover that Moses learned this lesson by the time he responded to God at the burning bush. God revealed Himself to Moses and called out to him, stating his name two times and then instructing Moses about his destiny.

> I have surely seen the affliction of My people who are in Egypt, and have given heed to their cry because of their taskmasters, for I am aware of their sufferings. So I have come down to deliver them from the power of the Egyptians (Exodus 3:7-8).

The Israelites had been crying and complaining 40 years earlier, but now they cried out to God. Moses hadn't been ready to be their deliverer, and they hadn't been ready to be delivered. It wasn't time yet. However, 40 years later, the right time had come.

> "Therefore, come now, and I will send you to Pharaoh, so that you may bring My people, the sons of Israel, out of Egypt." But Moses said to God, "*Who am I*, that I should go to Pharaoh, and that I should bring the sons of Israel out of Egypt?" (verses 10-11).

Notice that this is the same purpose Moses attempted to fulfill 40 years earlier—leading the Israelites out of bondage. God didn't change the purpose; He just changed the timing. You may feel as if God has always wanted you to do something, yet your life seems to be headed in another direction. Unless God changes your desire and burden to fulfill your purpose, keep holding on to it. It may simply be a matter of time. You may be in a period of development as God prepares you to carry out your purpose.

A Broken Spirit

Moses's response to God's call on his life the second time around reveals that he learned his lesson. He learned that God was the only One who could do what He said He would do. Moses didn't respond, "You're right, God, I'm the one. I'm the man. I'm going to go set my people free." Rather, he responded, "Who am I?" He later added, "Please, Lord, I have never been eloquent, neither recently nor in time past, nor since You have spoken to Your servant; for I am slow of speech and slow of tongue" (Exodus 4:10).

Moses didn't simply reply, "Um…who, me?" Rather, he said in effect, "You've got the wrong guy, God. Please—I'm not the one. I can't do this. In fact, I never could have done something like this."

This is the same Moses who four decades earlier had the money, background, history, culture, family name, education…and who decided to take care of the problem by himself. In fact, this is the Moses who, Stephen tells us, "was a man of power in words and deeds." The man who once had power in his words now says he can't even speak. In fact, he says he could never speak—that he must have had an enlarged ego and that he couldn't really do any of it well at all.

Moses is a broken man now. We are broken when God strips us of our self-sufficiency. Our confidence is no longer in ourselves. Any confidence we have is based on what we know God can do in us and through us. Confidence independent of God is unwise. It's a one-way ticket to herding sheep. I don't know of a man or woman who has been greatly used by God who didn't have to be stripped first. Every major character in the Bible whose life is unveiled before us had to go through a stripping process in the wilderness of development.

> Our confidence is based on what we know God can do in us and through us.

Development isn't fun, but it's necessary. Just as old furniture has to be stripped of its old shellac before it can be sanded down and refinished, we must endure the painful process of development. Moses was stripped until he knew he could never pull off his destiny on his own. He said, "Who am I, that I should go to Pharaoh, and that I should bring the sons of Israel out of Egypt?" (Exodus 3:11).

Bigger Than You Can Imagine

Here's an important clue to discovering your destiny: It will always be bigger than you. It will be more than you can even imagine. Moses knew he couldn't do a task this large alone. He had to ask, "How am I going to do this?" Friend, if you don't have to raise a similar question regarding your destiny, you might not yet know your destiny. Or you might know only a small part of it. God tells us in His Word, "Now to Him who is able to do far more abundantly beyond all that we ask or think, according to the power that works within us…" (Ephesians 3:20).

> Anything you can do on your own is too small to be God's destiny for you.

What might God want you to do that you know only He can do through you? If you can't think of anything like that in your life, you may never see what God can do. Anything you can do on your own is too small to be God's destiny for you. A small destiny doesn't require anything beyond your own natural resources.

In the wilderness, Moses had learned that he couldn't carry out his destiny on his own. In fact, Moses didn't think he could do it at all. And he certainly didn't think anyone would believe him when he showed up to do it.

> "Behold, I am going to the sons of Israel, and I will say to them, 'The God of your fathers has sent me to you.' Now they may say to me, 'What is His name?' What shall I say to them?" God said to Moses, "I AM WHO I AM"; and He said, "Thus you shall say to the sons of Israel, 'I AM has sent me to you'" (Exodus 3:13-14).

In those two words, God summed up who He was. In effect, He said, "I AM defined only by Myself. I am the eternally existing, self-generating One." *I* is a personal pronoun, and *Am* is present tense. In that name, God expresses His sufficiency. God told Moses that He is all Moses needs to fulfill his destiny.

Not only that, but God revealed His transcendence. Earlier He had said, "I am the God of Abraham," indicating that He is the God of Moses's past. In the next statement, He said, "I have surely seen the affliction of My people," revealing that He is also the God of Moses's present. And then He went on to say, "I have come down to deliver them," making sure that Moses knew He was also the God of his future.

His name, I AM, covered everything. It covered Moses's past, his present, and his future—just as God covers you.

> Ask God to show you your burning bush.

Moses took 40 years in the wilderness to learn the lesson of dependence. He required a setback in order to be set up for his destiny. But when his destiny arrived, God showed up in an extraordinary way.

If you have not yet walked into your destiny, or if you haven't yet received instructions for achieving and living out your purpose, or if you need further clarification from God, ask Him one thing. Ask Him to show you your burning bush. Ask Him to turn your ordinary wilderness experience into something extraordinary. When He does, turn aside to look, and you will hear Him call you by your name.

Moses's wilderness experience lasted 40 years. Yours doesn't have to. The lesson is often the same—allow God to strip you of your self-sufficiency so that He can accomplish His purpose through you.

Worship

13

I travel a lot. A typical week involves at least one flight to deliver the Word of God to a large group of people. When Sylvia (my assistant) and I began using cell phones, communication about my travel schedule and last-minute changes became a lot easier. But if you were to ask her, Sylvia could tell you about earlier times when reaching me at an airport wasn't so easy. Back in the day, communicating about changes in flights or hotels was more of a challenge.

One time, my fellow passengers and I were lining up to board a plane when I heard a faint voice over the public address system saying, "Tony Evans, please pick up a white courtesy phone." With all of the noise and chatter at an airport, I wasn't sure I had heard my name correctly, and I didn't know where a white courtesy phone might be. I had a flight to catch and was focused on getting ready to board. The plane wouldn't wait for me. But once again, I heard, "Tony Evans, please pick up a white courtesy phone."

When you hear your name being called in a situation like that, even if your flight is about to board, you stop. Thousands of people are at the airport, and if someone is calling you by name, the message must be important.

When I had heard my name the second time, I quickly got out of the boarding line and asked the attendant at the counter where a white courtesy phone was located. The agent behind the counter pointed to one, and I went to pick it up. I was glad I did—Sylvia was calling to let me know that because of a last-minute change in the schedule, I needed to board a different flight!

Minutes away from getting on an airplane that would have taken me to the wrong destination, I heard someone calling my name and directing me to a phone, where I received new information that put me on the path to where I needed to go.

What was I doing at the airport in the first place? I had gone to the airport to get where I thought I needed to go. But when I was about to board the plane that I thought would take me there, someone singled me out and called my name. And because that person called my name and I (eventually) responded, I received new instructions and altered my course so I could reach my destination and fulfill my purpose.

Friend, when you place yourself before God to worship Him—whether that be in your church, at home, on a walk, or wherever you direct your heart and mind to worship Him—you are on your way to a higher place. You are moving out of the earthly realm and into the heavenly realm. Worship lifts you from earth into heaven.

> Worship lifts you from earth into heaven.

When your passion is to leave this realm in order to enter that realm, don't be surprised if on your way, you hear your name. Don't be surprised if, as you begin to worship, your name is called and you are asked to "pick up a white courtesy phone." When you are in the right location of worship, God will often meet you where you are with a special instruction just for you. He will call your name. He will guide you. The Holy Spirit will speak to you. God will direct you.

But there's a catch. You must be able to hear Him.

Had I remained so focused on what I was doing—gathering my belongings, chatting with others in line, getting ready to board my flight—that I had tuned out the sounds around me, I would never have heard my name or received my instructions that day at the airport. As a result, I would have gone to the wrong destination.

Isaiah was worshipping God in the presence of angels when he heard God call his name and reveal the nature of his destiny. God said, "Whom shall I send, and who will go for Us?"

Isaiah quickly replied, "Here am I. Send me!" (Isaiah 6:8).

Hearing What Matters

One day, a Native American from a rural village decided to visit a friend in New York City. As they walked together down the bustling sidewalk, the Native American suddenly held up his hand. They paused, and he asked his friend, "Do you hear that?"

"Hear what?" his friend asked over the noise, a bit bewildered.

"It's a cricket," the Native American said.

"A cricket?" his friend replied. "I don't hear a cricket. In fact, how is it even possible to hear a cricket over the roar of the traffic?" The Native American then walked to the street corner, where a small cricket was sitting. He leaned over and scooped it up, much to the amazement of his friend.

The Native American smiled and led his friend toward a group of people. As they caught up with the group, he reached in his pocket, grabbed some change, and dropped it on the ground. Heads turned as the change hit the ground. Most of the people around them had heard the tiny sound.

> You hear what you want to hear.

The Native American turned toward his friend with a smile and said, "You hear what you want to hear."

When we don't hear God, the problem is not that He isn't talking, but that we're not attuned to the sound of His voice. God could stand before many of us and shout, yet we wouldn't hear Him simply because we wouldn't recognize His voice.

If you are pursuing your destiny, one basic necessity you must incorporate into your lifestyle is an attitude of worship. To worship God simply means to maintain a posture or mindset in which you intentionally and actively ascribe worth to God. To worship God is not only the right thing to do but also one of the most strategic investments you can make. As you acknowledge His infinite value and preeminence, you open yourself to a greater opportunity of communing with Him and, as a result, hearing directly from Him.

If you are searching for your destiny, or your calling, you need to be able to hear the caller. A calling always presumes a caller. You need to be able to hear the phone ring and know that He is on the line.

An event recorded for us in the book of Acts highlights two aspects of worship—the context and the content of your calling.

> Now there were at Antioch, in the church that was there, prophets and teachers: Barnabas, and Simeon who was called Niger, and Lucius of Cyrene, and Manaen who had been brought up with Herod the tetrarch, and Saul. While they were ministering to the Lord and fasting, the Holy Spirit said, "Set apart for Me Barnabas and Saul for the work to which I have called them." Then, when they had fasted and prayed and laid their hands on them, they sent them away (Acts 13:1-3).

The Context

The beginning of Acts 13 provides us with the context in which Paul and Barnabas received clear instruction as to their purpose. Both men were at Antioch, surrounded by other prophets and teachers. The church at Antioch included people from different cultures—the Greek term translated *Niger* meant "black," and Cyrene was an African nation. This church also included people from different classes—Manaen had been brought up with Herod the tetrarch and thus was originally from the royal community. When God calls us to unity in the body of Christ, He is not calling us all to be the same. Unity does not mean uniformity. Unity means oneness of purpose.

These men in the church at Antioch had one purpose. They were seeking to hear from God while worshipping Him, and they did not allow their differences to divide them. Rather, they gathered together with one purpose in mind—to hear from God.

We know they gathered together to hear from God because the passage describes them as prophets and teachers. In biblical times, prophets proclaimed the Word of God and applied its truth to the lives of the people. Teachers were pedagogues who made sure the people understood the Word of God. The church at Antioch was made up of leaders who communicated God's truth in a relevant way to the congregation.

They gathered not only to hear from God but also to worship Him. We read, "While they were ministering to the Lord and fasting, the Holy Spirit said…" (verse 2). To minister to the Lord is to worship Him, praise Him, and offer Him our service. Did you know that one of the main reasons you are to attend church and have personal times with God is to minister to Him? You engage in these practices not only so you will be ministered to yourself but also so you can minister to God.

In our churches and our personal times of worship, we need to be careful not to become so mechanical or scheduled that we program God right out of the picture. We have to be careful not to fill the time so much that we don't leave room for a fresh wind to blow or for the Holy Spirit to guide and direct our experience with Him.

The Holy Spirit's role is to communicate with God's people. Worship is one of the contexts in which He does this, as we see in Acts. Think of heaven as having a frequency, and think of worship as your antenna. Worship allows you to tune into heaven's frequency.

Most people don't have antennas these days because we live in a world of cable television, satellite dishes, and Internet feeds, but if you ever had an antenna, you probably had to move it and adjust it until you connected with the signal. When you connected with the signal, you saw a clear picture.

> Worship allows you to tune into heaven's frequency.

In worship, you adjust your spiritual antenna so you can receive the Holy Spirit's signal clearly. In this context, seeking God through His Word and in worship, Paul and Barnabas received specific instructions regarding their purpose.

Friend, don't be surprised if you discover your calling while you are seeking God through His Word at church, reading the Scripture, or listening to recorded sermons. Nearly every week I preach an hour-long sermon to thousands of people, most of whom I do not know on a deeply personal level. Yet without fail, people approach me after a service and tell me that the sermon had their name written all over it. They tell me that God spoke to them directly about something specific in their lives.

The beautiful thing about the Word of God is that one message can be applied thousands of ways to thousands of people because of the unique work of the Holy Spirit.

Have you heard a sermon that seemed to have your name in the title? "A Sermon Just for _____!" Perhaps you felt as if no one else were around and the teacher or preacher spoke directly to you. The Holy Spirit applied the generic truth directly to your specific situation.

God can speak to you in various ways. He can speak to you directly during your own personal time in His Word, but He may also speak to you through a preacher or teacher who proclaims God's truth. Either way, God will make His purpose for your life clear to your heart and mind when you seek Him with a heart of worship through His Word.

The Content

In the next verse in Acts 13, Paul and Barnabas experienced something that often happens to people today when they listen to a sermon or hear a message on God's Word. Paul and Barnabas received the content of their calling, and their names were written all over it. "The Holy Spirit said, 'Set apart for Me Barnabas and Saul for the work to which I have called them'" (verse 2). In other words, the Holy Spirit spoke.

The Bible does not explain how to apply everything it teaches to every unique setting. For example, it does not tell you where to work, whom to marry, or what your unique purpose might be.

We discover principles and precepts in the Bible. But we don't find all of the principles and precepts applied to specific circumstances. The Bible does not specifically address every person's unique situation. In order to make that application, we need more than the Bible—we need the guidance of the Holy Spirit.

But of course, we don't want to go so far as to say that all a person needs is the Holy Spirit and that the Bible is unimportant. The subjective experience of hearing from the Spirit cannot be compared with the objective experience of reading the truths in the Bible. The Holy Spirit will never say anything that contradicts the truths He wrote in the Bible. Scripture tells us that the words of God were recorded by the leading of the Holy Spirit (2 Peter 1:20-21). So anything the Spirit of God says to you will agree with what He wrote to you. He can't contradict Himself.

We are not to live in either extreme. We are to merge the two. The Holy Spirit guides, directs, enlightens, informs, leads, counsels, comforts, and more in the context of the truth of God's Word. Our human comprehension of spiritual truths is limited, but the Spirit guides us into all the truth (John 16:13).

> The subjective experience of hearing from the Spirit cannot be compared with the objective experience of reading the truths in the Bible.

One day, I was witnessing to a man and had given him an ironclad case for salvation. I laid out the whole thing, put Scriptures in all the right places, and assumed he was tracking with what I was saying. Just to make sure, I asked him to explain to me how someone becomes a Christian. That way I could see if he heard and understood the plan of salvation.

Yet each time I asked this man to explain how to become a Christian, he reverted back to what he believed and gave me all the wrong answers—going to church, doing good, and so on. Every time he gave me a wrong explanation, I started over again and worked through the whole concept step by step. After several unsuccessful attempts, I thought of Elisha asking God to open his servant's eyes so that he could see, and I did the same thing with this man. The problem definitely wasn't what the Bible said nor what I was saying. The problem was that there was too much fog cluttering his mind. He couldn't grasp it.

After I prayed, I started going through it again. But this time—halfway through—I saw a tremendous change in him. The light in his eyes brightened, and he got it. The Holy Spirit had illumined his mind so he could understand the spiritual truths he was hearing. When I asked him once again to tell me how a person becomes saved, he explained that Jesus had died and already paid the penalty for sin, that He had risen from the grave, and that a person simply needed to trust in Him and accept His payment personally. God had turned on the lightbulb.

He does the same thing with your destiny. You will know your destiny when you are living a lifestyle of worship, the lightbulb comes on, and you say, "I've got it! That's what I've been created to do!" The Holy Spirit will illumine your mind and reveal the deep truth of your purpose. It may be so deep, in fact, that it is difficult to articulate at first. You may know what it is but have trouble explaining it to others or even knowing exactly when and where you will have the opportunity to experience it. But you know beyond a shadow of a doubt that it is what you are supposed to do with the life you have been given. The Holy Spirit will have a job for you with your name on it...

...just as He did with Barnabas and Saul. Did you notice how specifically the Spirit spoke? He named Barnabas and Saul, and said He had a work for them to do. Your work, your purpose and destiny, has your name on it as well. And it is only for you to do. You have a unique calling. When you don't know what that is and you operate outside of your calling, you are attempting to do something you were never made to do.

> Your purpose and destiny has your name on it.

In order to hear God call your name, you need to listen for the still, small voice that comes in the midst of worshipping God and seeking Him through His Word. He speaks deeply to your spirit in a way unlike any other. And His words will never contradict the revelation of Scripture. Rather, the Bible will confirm the Spirit's message to you.

The closer you are to God, the less you have to manufacture in your life. The further you are from God, the more you have to manufacture. Why? Because the closer you are, the better you can hear Him and walk in His purpose for you. Your purpose may be unclear right now because you have not positioned yourself in a spirit of worship before God. When you develop a lifestyle of worship, you will hear Him. You will learn to recognize His voice calling your name.

Let God Drive

When my children were small, we went over to the church parking lot on a Saturday night when it was empty, and I let them "drive" the car. They each took a turn sitting on my lap and steering the wheel. But they didn't know that while they were driving, I was actually the one running the show. My foot was either on the brake or the accelerator, and regardless of where they had their hands on the wheel, I held the bottom of it with two fingers to control how far they could turn it. They weren't going to go too fast. Nor were they going to go anywhere they shouldn't.

In other words, they positioned themselves to go somewhere, but I controlled where they went. As a result, they had a much better experience than if they had driven on their own.

Friend, when you worship, you climb into God's lap and position yourself to go somewhere He wants to take you. You position yourself to have a brilliant ride in this life because you place yourself near Him, in His presence. You will never discover your destiny as long as you are functioning independently of God.

When you get close to Him, you will hear Him call you by name. That's what happened to Samuel. Samuel was in the house of the Lord, the temple, when he heard God call, "Samuel!" (1 Samuel 3:1-10).

God has a calling, a destiny, with your name on it. I don't know what it is. I can't tell you what it is. Don't write to me and ask me what it is because I'll just direct you back to God. But I do know that your destiny will always facilitate your passion, vision, gifts, experience, and opportunities. It will light a fire in you when you hear it, see it, or do it—such a fire that you would do it even if you weren't paid to do it simply because you were made to do it.

You will know your destiny when you hear the Spirit describe it and put your name on it. And when you do, embrace it with all you have within you. Enter into it as an act of worship toward God—to bring Him the glory that is due Him. After all, as we will see in the next chapter, to bring God glory is the result of living out your destiny.

Glory

Electromagnetic radiation is all around you. The air is thick with it. This radiation allows you to speak to someone on your cell phone, listen to the radio, receive a television signal through your satellite dish, or operate your computer wirelessly.

No one can see this electromagnetic radiation in our atmosphere. What you see or hear, rather, is its effect. You see what it produces.

Scripture tells us that no man has seen God at any time. God is invisible to our human eyes. He is a Spirit—an essence that our eyes are not able to visualize. Yet the atmosphere weighs heavy with His presence because God is everywhere.

When God's invisible reality comes across in living color to His creation, the result is simply called His glory. God's glory reflects God Himself. It is the visible manifestation of the invisible attributes of God.

The Old Testament idea of glory comes from a number of Hebrew terms. It is best understood through three of them. The first is the Hebrew word *kâbôd*, which is derived from the original root *kâbad*, meaning "heavy," "weighty," and "honor." The second component of God's glory comes from the Hebrew word *hâdâr*. When combined with its root, *hâdâr* means "to swell," "swelling," "splendor," and "ornament." The third major aspect comes from the Hebrew word *hâlal*, which means "shine," "praise," and "praiseworthy."

When we combine these thoughts, we see that glory is the weighty, shining splendor of God. He is the weightiest, heaviest, deepest Being in the universe. To glorify Him or to speak of His glory is to enter into and engage that which is invisible through that which can now be seen and experienced. We see God's glory when He shows up and reveals Himself in a way that evokes a response of praise.

Unlike everyone else, God is intrinsically glorious. Everyone else has ascribed glory. We honor police officers, military personnel, and government officials because of their positions and duties. Take off the uniform and badge, remove the title and duties, and those people would not receive the glory they had received before. When a judge puts on a robe and takes his place, we ascribe glory to him. Take off the robe, and he's just another man walking down the street.

God isn't like that. He is intrinsically glorious regardless of whether we ascribe glory to Him. God is glorious because He's glorious. Similarly, water is wet because it's wet. You can't discuss water without discussing wetness because wetness is part of the intrinsic nature of water. Similarly, you can't discuss the sun without discussing blazing heat because blazing heat is part of the intrinsic nature of the sun. Whether you are happy about water being wet or the sun being blazing hot is irrelevant. Those attributes are intrinsic to water and the sun.

Likewise, God is glorious intrinsically. When you recognize His glory, He is glorious. When you don't recognize His glory, He is still glorious. When you like His glory, He is glorious. When you don't care one way or the other about His glory, He is still glorious. God is glorious simply because that's the way He is.

> When you fulfill your destiny, you tap into the glory of God.

Here's one of the greatest things about fulfilling your destiny: You get to intentionally tap into the glory of God. As we saw in an earlier chapter, the chief end of man is to glorify God and to enjoy Him forever.

To state it plainly, whatever you think about God, He is much more than that and then some. God's glory is greater than all of His creation. Keep in mind that the earth is only a small portion of creation. God created a universe that mankind cannot even comprehend. And God is even more than that.

Almost everything God created automatically recognizes His glory.

- "Since the creation of the world His invisible attributes, His eternal power and divine nature, have been clearly seen, being understood through what has been made, so that they are without excuse" (Romans 1:20).
- "From Him and through Him and to Him are all things. To Him be the glory forever. Amen" (Romans 11:36).
- "...everyone who is called by My name, and whom I have created for My glory, whom I have formed, even whom I have made" (Isaiah 43:7).

Unfortunately, two things don't recognize God's glory: Satan and his angels, and fallen humanity. Many people do not know their purpose because they have missed the fundamental premise that life is not about them. It's about Him. God says, "I have created you for My glory." He created you to be the television or radio station that broadcasts His invisible attributes. He created you to reflect Him.

The problem is that most of us are anthropocentric rather than theocentric. That is, we are man-centered rather than God-centered. Many people are existentialists, for whom the central focus of life is human experience and free will. An existentialist asks, what is my destiny by me for me? Most of these people do not openly claim to be existentialists, and they may not even know that their lives reflect this belief system, but it is the most common worldview in the Western world today.

God wants you to ask a different question. Don't ask, what is your destiny by you for you? Ask instead, what is your destiny by God for God? You were created to reflect Him and His glory to a world in desperate need of seeing, experiencing, and feeling Him and His glory.

I have been a pastor for more than 36 years, and I have witnessed a trend in the church that saddens me—individuals coming to church to be blessed. They come to church wanting to know what the church is going to do for them. They want to know what is in it for them. Nothing is wrong with being blessed, but the problem comes when individuals focus on their own blessing. They neglect the higher purpose of allowing that blessing to touch others and reflect God's glory.

When we bless others, we reflect God's glory.

Focusing on our own blessing leads to frustration, depression, and emptiness because God created each of us for Himself. When we bless others, we reflect God's glory. Both the giver and the receiver are blessed. Yet when our lives are all about ourselves and not about Him, we miss the experience of God's glory that comes through blessing others.

God created you for His glory. He brings you pleasure when you reflect His pleasure. Why should God give you His purpose for your life if you're not sure whose glory you are seeking to reflect?

The Greatest Glory

We can always focus on God because no one is greater than Him. On your best day, someone is still greater than you. You may be pretty, but someone is still prettier. You may be smart, but someone is smarter. You may be wealthy, but someone is wealthier. Yet when God looks for someone greater than Himself, He finds no one at all. No one is greater than God. Thus nothing and no one deserves more glory than Him.

You can tell whether people have a heart for God by whose glory they are seeking—His or their own. This is the starting point for Christian growth: "Grow in the grace and knowledge of our Lord and Savior Jesus Christ. To Him be the glory, both now and to the day of eternity. Amen" (2 Peter 3:18). The desire and drive to reflect God's glory is an indicator of spiritual growth. If you are seeking more glory for yourself and God is getting less glory in your life, you are moving in the wrong spiritual direction. As you grow in living out your purpose, your passion for His name, His glory, and His recognition will increase.

The reverse of that is true as well. Sin can increase in people's lives even if they never go out and rob a bank. Sin is frequently increasing when people try to take the glory that belongs only to God. In Isaiah we read, "I am the LORD, that is My name; I will not give My glory to another" (Isaiah 42:8). When you try to take God's glory for yourself, you are a cosmic thief. Whatever God has blessed you with—intellect, looks, wealth, or your gregarious personality—God is to receive the glory because God is the One who has given it to you. Sin dominates our thoughts and our lives when we keep for ourselves the glory and visible recognition God demands and deserves.

> As you grow in living out your purpose, your passion for His name, His glory, and His recognition will increase.

The All-Encompassing Glory of God

Many of our problems today stem from the fact that we are not consumed with God's glory. We will dip into it for a little bit on a Sunday morning and possibly a Wednesday night. Or we might try to access it by watching a television preacher or participating in a Bible study. But notice how the book of Revelation describes the all-encompassing nature of God's glory, which we will one day experience in its fullness in heaven: "The city has no need of the sun or of the moon to shine on it, for the glory of God has illumined it, and its lamp is the Lamb" (Revelation 21:23). If God's unleashed and visible glory shines brighter than the sun in heaven, there certainly must be plenty of it to reach earth right now.

Rather than giving God's glory a nod or a song or a two-hour block of time on a Sunday, bask in God's all-consuming presence now. The closer you get to God, the closer you get to experiencing the power and purpose of His glory.

Moses asked God to show him His glory.

> Moses said, "I pray You, show me Your glory!" And He said, "I Myself will make all My goodness pass before you,

and will proclaim the name of the LORD before you…"
But He said, "You cannot see My face, for no man can
see Me and live!" Then the LORD said, "Behold, there is a
place by Me, and you shall stand there on the rock; and it
will come about, while My glory is passing by, that I will
put you in the cleft of the rock and cover you with My
hand until I have passed by. Then I will take My hand
away and you shall see My back, but My face shall not be
seen" (Exodus 33:18-23).

In essence, God said that when He passed by, He would let Moses
see His exhaust fumes because if He allowed Moses to look directly at
Him and His glory, Moses would not be able to live. It might be similar to being exposed to a nuclear reaction—Moses would disintegrate
from the weight of what he experienced. This is why when you and I
go to heaven, we will receive new, glorified bodies. These new bodies
will be able to receive and experience God's glory in its fullness.

Moses was allowed to see just a sliver of God's glory on earth because
a sliver was all he could handle. God's glory is powerful. Something so
powerful, important, and weighty should be taken seriously. So when
God says we have been created for His glory, He gives us an awesome
assignment. We have an incredible privilege—God allows us, and in
fact intentionally chooses us, to reflect His splendorous glory. Your
purpose is to be a physical, visible, historical reflection of what will one
day consume and embrace us in eternity. We are to touch heaven by
radiating God's glory on earth.

Glorifying God Through Sacrifice

We best glorify God by doing what He tells us to do and not simply what we want to do. Jesus says, "I glorified You on the earth, having accomplished the work which You have given Me to do" (John
17:4). Glorifying God and fulfilling your destiny are directly connected.

Last year, God gave me the job of serving the Dallas Cowboys as
their chaplain, and I gave Him glory by doing the work He gave me
to do. But doing that work didn't cost me anything personally. In fact,

I was more than happy to fulfill the requirements of that task. I loved that assignment. The tricky part is giving God glory by doing what He has asked you to do when it costs you something, such as your freedom, your personal wants, your comfort, or your pride.

> We best glorify God by doing what He tells us to do and not simply what we want to do.

As Jesus was preparing to be taken to the cross and crucified for the sins of all mankind, He said something very revealing about how we are to glorify God. "Now My soul has become troubled; and what shall I say, 'Father, save Me from this hour'? But for this purpose I came to this hour. Father, glorify Your name" (John 12:27-28).

Jesus didn't mince words. He didn't sugarcoat His feelings. Jesus's soul was troubled. He wanted to ask God to save Him from this hour. Jesus hoped God would not make Him go through with what was about to happen. But then He turned it all around because what He was about to experience was directly tied to His purpose and God's glory. "Go ahead, God," Jesus said. "This is why I came. Glorify Your name."

Even though Jesus wanted a way out, He finished the work He had been sent to do because He knew that in His purpose—in fulfilling the work God had intended for Him, however painful it was—He was bringing glory to God.

Are you in a relationship with God for His sake or for your own sake? God will reveal your motives by allowing a day of trouble. You won't want things to be going the way they are going. You won't want things to be working out the way they are working out. You won't want to go down that path. You won't want to take that road. You won't want to go there, do that, or experience that situation. You'll know the steps ahead of you will be painful—but you'll take them anyway because that is what He asked you to do.

All of us could glorify God if He were to send us a million dollars, give us new houses, solve all our problems, or make our work situations turn around in our favor. Anyone can do that. But God wants to know if we will glorify Him when we have to pick up our crosses and follow Him. What happens when we don't get the promotion? What happens when we get overlooked on the job? What happens when our spouses walk out on us? Our children rebel? The doctor doesn't give us the report that we wanted to hear? What happens then? Do we still do what He has asked us to do? Do we still hang in there? Do we still walk down the path He has shown us? Or do we throw in the towel, quit, and leave?

God wants to know—are you in this for you, or are you in this for Him? The tragedy today is that most of us are usually in it for ourselves. When the pain and disappointments of life show up, we want to fix them, change them, or leave them altogether. All the while our faith and praise quickly diminish into a mere whisper.

> Are you in this for you, or are you in this for Him?

God didn't save you just to take you to heaven. God saved you so that earth would have a living, breathing HD reflection of His glory. That is why Job said, "Though He slay me, I will hope in Him" (Job 13:15). Job didn't back down from stating his case, arguing his points, and making his complaints to God. But he also stood corrected at the end of the day. He was willing to be corrected because of what he affirmed: "I will hope in Him." In essence, he was venting to God. But when all was said and done, Job said, "I lay my hand on my mouth" (Job 40:4). I trust You.

Habakkuk also suffered. After enduring enemy oppression, despair, and scarcity, he summed up his experience by saying this:

> Though the fig tree should not blossom
> And there be no fruit on the vines,
> Though the yield of the olive should fail
> And the fields produce no food,
> Though the flock should be cut off from the fold
> And there be no cattle in the stalls,
> Yet I will exult in the LORD,

I will rejoice in the God of my salvation.
The Lord GOD is my strength,
And He has made my feet like hinds' feet,
And makes me walk on my high places (Habakkuk 3:17-19).

When you shift the way you view your purpose and God's glory—just as Job and Habakkuk did—you gain God's undivided attention. God restored more to Job than he had lost. Habakkuk walked on high places above the situation and the others around him. Jesus rose from the dead and is seated at the right hand of God as the King of kings and the Lord of lords.

Glory to Glory

Once you view all of your life—the good, the bad, and the bitter—through the grid of God's glory, everything changes.

And look what happens next. "We all, with unveiled face, beholding as in a mirror the glory of the Lord, are being transformed into the same image from glory to glory, just as from the Lord, the Spirit" (2 Corinthians 3:18). Make this decision to unveil your face, heart, and spirit—your soul—before God. Remove the layers of self-preservation, protection, and pride, and authentically trust Him. When you do, you will be transformed. His glory will rest on you and thus become your glory.

You will be like Moses, who was transparent in God's presence for an extended period of time. When he returned to his people, "the sons of Israel would see the face of Moses, that the skin of Moses' face shone" (Exodus 34:35). God's glory was all over Moses. The longer Moses stayed away from God, the more God's glory faded, and Moses's face would no longer shine as brightly until he returned to God's presence.

Yet 2 Corinthians reminds us that we are not like Moses because we are living under the new covenant, and God's glory now transforms us continually from the inside. God's glory is to radiate inside of you so much that you will have a glow that does not depend on your circumstances. Your glow won't have anything to do with your situation.

Instead, you will glow because you are embracing God's purpose in your life—to glorify Him by trusting Him even in situations you cannot understand and do not want to experience.

If you want to know your destiny, live for God's glory even in the daily and mundane things of life (1 Corinthians 10:31). When you live for His glory, He'll reveal your destiny. But He's not going to show it to you if you don't first respect His presence. Once you get that straight, you don't need to knock yourself out trying to track down your destiny. You don't need to go to the ends of the earth to locate your destiny.

If you want to know your destiny, live for God's glory.

Once you determine that you will live for God's glory regardless of what you want to do, feel, or experience, God will bring your destiny to you. As we read earlier, "Seek first His kingdom and His righteousness, and all these things will be added to you" (Matthew 6:33). Jesus didn't say, "Seek first His kingdom and His righteousness [in other words, His glory], and then go and seek all the other things too." No, when you seek God's kingdom and glory first, all the other things will be added to you. They come to you. God takes responsibility to provide all you need to do whatever He wants you to do. You won't have to break your neck to get it. You won't have to wear yourself out trying to accomplish it. God will cause it to flow naturally to you because, after all, He will receive the glory. God doesn't mind picking up the tab to bring your destiny your way when He knows that you will do it no matter what and that He will get the glory.

Before you take another step toward discovering your destiny, you have a decision to make. For whose glory will you live? Will you live for your name, your reputation, your recognition, your exaltation, and your 15 minutes of fame? If that's what you want, that's all you'll get, and trust me, 15 minutes of fame is still only 15 minutes in light of eternity. It's not going to last that long.

Or are you going to live for the eternal King, who rules over an eternal kingdom? His destiny for you includes you and benefits you but has been designed to advance His kingdom on earth, bless others, and reflect His greatest glory.

Reflected Glory

Many a man has walked a beautiful lady outside on a full moonlit night and pointed up at the moon. There's something romantic about a full moon against the backdrop of a darkened sky. But if you will recall from your science classes, the moon has no light of its own. The moon is dark 24 hours a day, seven days a week. When we look at the moon, we see the brilliant reflection of the even more brilliant sun. The radiant moon does no work on its own. Rather, it reflects the work of the sun in all its glory because the moon produces no light.

The problem is that sometimes something gets in the way. Actually, the earth gets in the way. Whenever only part of the moon is lit up, Earth is blocking the sun's glory. The sun is still there to light the whole moon, but because of the way Earth and moon rotate, Earth sometimes blocks the sun's light from reflecting off of the full moon.

Friend, what are you allowing to get in the way of God's glory and reduce your ability to be a full reflection of Him? What is standing between you and God's desire to have you reflect full hope, full direction, full power, and full peace? Only after you realize that you are created to reflect God and that your life is about Him will you be able to fully live out your destiny. If you don't, you will join the countless millions who simply go through life existing day by day and who will one day stand before their Creator in heaven, only to hear Him say, "I had so much that I wanted to accomplish through you. I had so much that I wanted to do through you. I had so much that I wanted to show you, but I never could get you to focus your full and undivided attention on My glory. You wanted your own."

Friend, it's really all about His glory.

And in case you didn't hear me (it's so important I'm going to say it again), your destiny is about His glory.

Future

15

I have talked with many people over the years who seem to be living with a sense of hopelessness. Questions like these bounce around in their heads: Am I ever going to get where I'm supposed to be? Am I ever going to do what I'm supposed to do? Is life ever going to work for me? These people have lost a sense of hope. They have lost a sense of destiny.

Friend, if that sounds like you today, I have a good verse for you to encourage you on your journey. It's located in a difficult chapter of a difficult book—a ray of hope surrounded by clouds of discouragement. Perhaps that is how you feel today. You may feel as if you endure bad day after bad day, bad year after bad year, or even bad decade after bad decade. Yet even though this verse is surrounded by despair and hopelessness, it offers just the opposite. It offers hope, meaning, and purpose. You too can discover your destiny even in the midst of despair.

"'I know the plans that I have for you,' declares the LORD, 'plans for welfare and not for calamity to give you a future and a hope'" (Jeremiah 29:11). That is God's promise just for you.

Many of us make New Year's resolutions, and most of us break them. They may include being a better person, eating better, working out at the gym, memorizing Scripture, or watching less football. A resolution is simply a firm decision to do something. It's a decree or a promise. Every January, our resolutions resound with determination and the hope of new beginnings. By May, their nagging presence reminds us that we didn't quite reach our goals. By December, most of us have forgotten what we resolved to do.

You may or may not join with the millions who make New Year's resolutions, but I want to remind you that there is One who has kept every resolution He has ever made. He keeps His promises. He keeps His Word.

And even if we are not able to stick it out in the gym, stay away from the chocolate, or bite our tongue rather than beat others with it—He is able to do exceeding, abundantly above all we could ever imagine. And He has resolved that your life is going to be a *great* life. It is a life filled with "a future and a hope." The surest way to live out your destiny is to fix your eyes on the unchanging faithfulness of the One who has promised that goodness and loving-kindness will follow you when you follow Him (Psalm 23:6).

Your life may hold some surprises, but I know who holds your life. And He says that you are to be of good cheer because He has already overcome it all. If He has overcome it, then you, His child and as His heir, have overcome it too.

I understand how easily we can get caught up in the circumstances of life. Things can seem overwhelming. I understand how easily we can lose hope. But if you will keep your eyes fixed on the Lord and not on your circumstances, you will see that He who began a good work in you will also complete it.

People lose hope when they can't see a future. Yesterday was bleak, today is still bleak, and tomorrow doesn't look any better. The weather report of their lives says, "No sunshine." Nothing out there has their number on it or seems related to their calling or destiny.

If you are one of those people, memorize and meditate on Jeremiah 29:11. This great verse from a difficult chapter in an equally difficult book is for all those who feel they are having bad lives. God brought a promise of hope to the Israelites while they were still in captivity in Babylon. Verse 4 tells us, "Thus says the LORD of hosts, the God of Israel, to all the exiles whom I have sent into exile from Jerusalem to Babylon..." The Israelites had been sent into exile. They would be under

God's judgment and disciplining hand for 70 years. To make it worse, the place they had been sent to was as pagan as could be. Babylon was not where the believers hung out. It was an evil and idolatrous place, a terrible place to live—particularly if you were an Israelite. These people were in a desperate situation full of negative circumstances, pagan influences, and divine judgment. Yet in the midst of this discouragement, hopelessness, and pain, God shows up and says, "I know the plans I have for you."

Why is that so important? Because when God says He has a plan, you know the story isn't over. In fact, you are still here, so your life isn't over. Your destiny is not over. Your purpose is not over. Your calling is not over. You are still living, breathing, and functioning on planet earth, so God still has a plan just for you.

> When God says He has a plan, you know the story isn't over.

You may be saying, "But, Tony, you don't know about my past. It's messed up—God would never use me." Well, Israel had a past too. Yet God still had a plan for them that included a future and a hope. Remember, some of your greatest lessons about faith and humility will be learned in the dark. These are the times when you feel so hopeless that you don't know what in the world God is doing, how He is doing it, and why He is taking so long. God may be silent, but He is not still. When you feel furthest from Him, He is the closest He'll ever be. One of the key components of a life of destiny is trust in the Lord in times that don't make sense.

I know your life may look dark, the path may seem unclear, and you might have no idea where God is taking you. In fact, it may be pitch black outside. But if you are in one of those times right now, hold on because when God moves, you will move. Maybe He's stopped at the corner of your life right now because there is too much traffic coming. I don't know the reason why He has allowed you to be stuck, delayed, or seemingly hindered from living out your destiny right at this very moment. But if He has, I do know this—He has a plan for you, and it is a good plan to give you both a future and a hope.

In the Meantime

God tells you what to do while you are waiting to realize your destiny, just as He told the Israelites. Earlier in the chapter, He instructed them, "Build houses and live in them; and plant gardens and eat their produce...Seek the welfare of the city where I have sent you into exile, and pray to the LORD on its behalf; for in its welfare you will have welfare" (Jeremiah 29:5,7).

Waiting on the timing of your destiny is not the same as sitting back and doing nothing. God says to become as productive as you possibly can where you are. Do all that is in your hand to do. Maximize everything that is set before you. Seize the moment right where you are. While waiting on God for your destiny, promote the well-being of the people around you now. Even if you are not where you want to be or if you are not doing what you want to do, benefit those around you. Invest in them and increase the well-being of their lives. Surely the Israelites were not happy about their captivity in Babylon, but God instructed them to pray for the Babylonians and work for their betterment. He told them that in the Babylonians' well-being they would find their own. God would bless them for being a blessing to others.

Many of us choose to do nothing while waiting on God to bring about a change in our lives or get us out of difficult situations. But the only time you are to do nothing is when there is nothing to do. If there is nothing you can do, then do nothing. But if God has given you something to do where you are right now, do it with all your might. Invest in your surroundings right now. Seek the well-being of those around you. As you become a blessing to others, you set yourself up to be blessed. As you help others locate and live out their destinies, you set yourself up to discover your own.

> As you help others locate and live out their destinies, you set yourself up to discover your own.

People often lose hope because they are concerned only about themselves. If you are messed up and all you can see is you, you are perpetuating your own decline. In spite of the

Israelites' circumstances, they were to be productive on behalf of others. They were to invest in other people's lives. And God promised to invest in their own lives as well.

> "Then you will call upon Me and come and pray to Me, and I will listen to you. You will seek Me and find Me when you search for Me with all your heart. I will be found by you," declares the LORD, "and I will restore your fortunes and will gather you from all the nations and from all the places where I have driven you," declares the LORD, "and I will bring you back to the place from where I sent you into exile" (Jeremiah 29:12-14).

Many Christians read and quote Jeremiah 29:11 without fully understanding the context. What brought God to the point of saying what He did? Without knowing the answer to that question, readers throw out the principles in the rest of the passage, and they don't experience the truth of verse 11. Rather than searching for God with all their hearts, as verse 12 tells us to do, people search for the solution to their problem or meaning in their destiny with all of their heart. They search for the wrong thing, so they don't find it. God says that He has the plan. He has *your* plan. He doesn't want you to go looking for the plan—He wants you to go searching for Him. When you find Him, you will find the plan as well because He knows what it is and wants to give it to you.

God has a plan for you. He has a destiny for you. Maybe you should have gotten it earlier in your life. Maybe you shouldn't have done this or that or the other thing that got you off track. Or maybe if someone else hadn't done something to you, you would have gotten it earlier. Maybe if you had gotten saved earlier, hadn't married that person out of God's will, hadn't sought a career out of His will, or hadn't just been plain rebellious, maybe you would

> God doesn't want you to go looking for the plan—He wants you to go searching for Him.

have reached your destiny earlier. Regardless, God has a plan for you. And it's a good plan, filled with a future and a hope.

Israel would not see God's plan for 70 years. The prophets were falsely telling them about their deliverance (Jeremiah 14:14; 29:8-9). But the prophets didn't know what they were talking about. They just said whatever the people wanted to hear. God knew the exile would last longer than they thought. That's why He told them to be as productive as they could right where they were until they saw Him do what He said He would do.

The Israelites didn't like being in bondage, and I'm sure you don't like being in the dark about your destiny. Your best course of action is to seek God. "Without faith it is impossible to please Him, for he who comes to God must believe that He is and that He is a rewarder of those who seek Him" (Hebrews 11:6). If you don't know which way to go, seek Him. If you are in pain, seek Him. If you are confused, seek Him. If you are waiting, seek Him. If you track me down and ask me which way you are supposed to go, I'm going to send you back to Him because He has not told me His plan for you. Seek Him, and in the process, you will discover your destiny.

Sometimes God will seem to be doing nothing. Yet He often works invisibly—behind the scenes—by turning yesterday's pains into tomorrow's peace. God is asking you to take hold of His hand and never let go because He knows where He is taking you. He is leading you to a good, wonderful place because it has a future and a hope. What God starts, God finishes. What God begins, God ends. What God initiates, God completes. You may be saying, "Tony, I'm in a bigger mess right now than you can imagine." To which I reply, "My God is even bigger—bigger than you can imagine."

If you forget everything else you've read in this book so far, remember this verse: "'I know the plans that I have for you,' declares the Lord, 'plans for welfare and not for calamity to give you a *future* and a *hope*.'"

You have a destiny—a good destiny. Seek Him, and you will find it.

CONCLUSION

Soldiers, looking more like robots than men, lined the streets and the stadiums. Not by the thousands who would later attempt to conquer the world, but by the dozens. Just enough to send chills down the spines of anyone these would-be rulers deemed unfit to be called human.

But even these soldiers couldn't prevent the gathering of athletes from a myriad of countries to take part in the largest global athletic competition, the Olympics.

The year was 1936. Going to a movie would cost 15 cents—a car, no more than $600. Babe Ruth had recently laid down his bat, and a young man who would one day be known as Joltin' Joe had carried his to the plate for the first time. Greta Garbo dominated the screen, and FDR continued trying to pick up the pieces of the US economy after the Great Depression.

Despite rigid segregation in the United States, a black man now stood on enemy soil as his country's top contender for three gold medals.

By Hitler's definition, he wasn't human. And maybe Hitler was right because what this man had accomplished a year earlier in Ann Arbor—setting three world records and tying a fourth in 45 minutes—had seemed superhuman. No man has come close to doing the same again.

Born the grandson of slaves and the son of a sharecropper, he was named James Cleveland Owens after his father in 1913. James's name was changed, however, to Jesse when he told a teacher it was J.C. His new name, Jesse, interestingly enough, is derived from the Hebrew *Yishai*, which means "God exists" and "God's gift."

Jesse was no doubt a gift to those he represented in America and to his family in 1936. Grabbing gold medals in the long jump and the 100- and 200-meter sprints, he mastered his race in front of the man who had made the claim that there was only one master race in existence. Later, the host country pressured the Americans to pull their Jewish competitors from the final relay. So a few days after Jesse had earned what he had thought was his final gold medal of the 1936 Olympics, he was penciled in to run the first leg of the 4 x 100 men's relay.

Neither Jesse nor his teammate, Ralph Metcalfe, had practiced passing the baton the entire time they had been at the Olympics. The relay wasn't a common race for either of them. Yet with little time for preparation, they took to the track, determined to do the best they could with what they had. They were determined to fulfill their destiny.

Jesse not only managed to stay in his lane and run faster than his competitors, he passed the baton seamlessly on his way to grabbing his fourth gold of the games and another world record.

Jesse had competed both personally and corporately in a hostile foreign realm, yet he had come out on top. Battling in enemy territory and despite harsh segregation from within and without, Jesse stood on the highest podium more times than any of the others. His unwavering confidence in who he was created to be and what he had been created to do gave his family and his nation a reason to be proud. In fact, the host country recently honored this man's prowess by naming a street after him.

Friend, you may never run in the Olympic games the way Jesse Owens did. And most likely, you will never own your own Olympic gold medals. But just as Jesse represented his country in a hostile nation, you have a destiny that involves representing God's kingdom in a hostile world. As a believer, you have been called to run your race in enemy land. You have been chosen to aim for the gold, having been given everything you need to get it.

The leader of the enemy coalition stands by watching. He declared your defeat before your race even began. His followers line the streets and the stadium of your heart and mind, daring you to prove their leader wrong. They don't think you can.

And now, as one of God's chosen people grafted into His body, you have been asked to substitute in the relay. You have been called on to run—not just for yourself or for your country, but for all who come after you in this race.

To pass the kingdom baton.

When Jesse jumped at the 1936 Olympics, he jumped for himself and for his country. When he ran the two sprints, he did the same. But when Jesse darted down the first leg of the 4 x 100 men's relay, he also ran for those who came after him that day. Because the key to winning any relay is to pass the baton well. It is to connect with the next runner seamlessly. Victory is in how well you position him to run.

Living out your destiny involves your personal races in life. It involves your family and your church. But after you do all of those things well, it also involves passing the baton, helping members of the next generation to live out their destinies as well in the kingdom of God.

Your destiny is about much more than just you. It is part of the puzzle that includes others living out their destinies too. Had Jesse not run in the relay that day, the other three runners may not have grabbed their gold. Living up to your destiny is a God-given responsibility that includes your talents, skills, passion, experiences, and so much more. God links all of these together as His gift to you in order to enable you to live your life as a gift to Him and to others.

You have a destiny. Seize it. It is yours for the taking.

QUESTIONS FOR DISCUSSION AND PERSONAL REFLECTION

Introduction

1. Dr. Evans says, "Many of God's children have turned on their Creator. Rather than live for Him, they choose to live for themselves." Are you ever tempted to live for yourself? In what ways?

2. Have you ever tried to be someone else? Who? How did you try to be like that person?

Chapter 1: Concept

1. "God placed mankind on earth to serve as His stewards over His creation...God has designed you to have all that you need to productively rule your world." In what ways can you be God's steward in your world? In other words, what does it mean for you to productively rule your world?

2. You are rare, special, valuable...God's masterpiece! List a few of your unique characteristics.

3. How might God use those characteristics to spread His kingdom? What hints do these give you about your God-given destiny?

Chapter 2: Kingdom

1. In what ways can you personally seek first the kingdom of God?

2. Do you ever struggle with seeking other things before seeking the kingdom of God? What things?

3. "If He is truly before all things, He will hold all things together." What is God holding together in your life? What do you need Him to hold together?

4. "God saved you not just so you can go to heaven—which will be great!—but so that He could fulfill His purpose through you on earth." Should going to heaven be your ultimate goal? Why or why not?

Chapter 3: Rationale

1. Relate a time when you felt wonderfully fulfilled. Why might you have felt that way in that situation?

2. Complete this sentence: I will know I have been successful when...

3. Do you have a clear sense of direction in a particular part of your life? Do you need direction? Share some examples.

Chapter 4: Completeness

1. Dr. Evans writes about being energized when he preaches. Can you think of a topic, activity, need, or goal that energizes you? Can you think of a time you were energized by doing something? Explain.

2. "Everything you do has now become kingdom activity, even if you once considered it to be secular. There is no distinction between the secular and the sacred when you are a kingdom-minded person." List a few seemingly secular parts of your life that have now become sacred.

Chapter 5: Intention

1. "[God] is sovereign over everything, including the creation of life. This means that nothing comes to you that does not pass through God's fingers first—including your very existence." List a couple challenging situations in your life. Did they pass through God's fingers before they reached you? Why is that an important question to consider?

2. "In order to live your life calmly, you must fully embrace God's sovereignty rather than question everything." Are you living calmly? Think of an area in which you would like to be calmer. Speak or write a sentence or two expressing God's sovereignty in that area.

3. What adjustments have you had to make in order to live in God's kingdom?

Chapter 6: Passion

1. What are you most passionate about? How do you express that passion?

2. What seemingly meaningless or mundane activities in your life are actually helping you to someday fulfill your passion?

3. What would you like to do if you had all the money and time you needed?

4. What would you attempt if you knew that you could not possibly fail?

Chapter 7: Vision

1. Abraham was blessed to be a blessing. Name one blessing God has given *to* you that He wants to use to bless others *through* you.

2. Have you ever had to take a bold step in order to follow God's leading? Share one example if you can.

3. Do you have a dream? What do you hope to be experiencing a year from now, five years from now, or ten years from now?

4. Dr. Evans writes, "If something on your heart burdens you or evokes strong emotions in you, before you try to talk yourself out of those feelings or rationalize them, ask God if they are clues to your vision and your destiny." What evokes strong emotions in you? How might that lead you to God's vision for your life?

Chapter 8: Giftedness

1. Have you ever sensed God's anointing—a time when He empowered you to be more effective than you could have been on your own? Share an example if you can.

2. Dr. Evans writes that we will one day have to answer the question, how did you utilize the gifts given to you to further God's kingdom on earth? What is one way you can utilize one of your gifts to further God's kingdom?

3. Dr. Evans writes, "God gave you your spiritual gifts so you can be a blessing to others." Have you ever began serving others, only to find out that you were as blessed in the process as they were? Share an example.

Chapter 9: Experience

1. What positive thing in your life—such as a relationship, an educational experience, a job, or a well-honed skill—can you use to further God's kingdom?

2. Have you made a mistake that God has turned around— or that you hope He can turn around—to help you fulfill your purpose in life?

3. Name one bitter situation that you have suffered. How might God turn that around to help you experience your

destiny? Do you need to cooperate with God by asking Him to help you forgive someone?

Chapter 10: Intersections

1. Dr. Evans writes, "We begin discovering our divine intersections when we seek God in the midst of our normal, everyday events." He later writes, "When you include God in your routine, the natural becomes supernatural. You discover your destiny when the natural merges with the divine." Name one part of your normal routine. How can you include God in it or seek God in the midst of it?

2. Dr. Evans writes, "You absolutely must have people in your life who won't let you quit." Can you think of someone like that in your life—a friend, a teacher, a coworker, a pastor…?

3. Share an example of God speaking a word to you. Did it come through a sermon, a conversation, a time of reflection, a Bible passage…?

Chapter 11: Commitment

1. The apostle Paul encourages us to make the most of our time, or as the King James puts it, to redeem the time. Share one specific way you can apply that instruction to your life.

2. What is the first thing that comes to your mind when you read that you are to present yourself to God as a living sacrifice?

3. "When the Holy Spirit transforms your mind, He replaces your old, worldly way of thinking with His thoughts." Have you ever realized that you had been believing a lie about yourself or your circumstances? Share an example of God's thoughts replacing your worldly thoughts.

Chapter 12: Development

1. Have you ever gone through a valley of development? Are you in one now? Explain.

2. Moses's initial plan to deliver his fellow Hebrews backfired because his timing was off. Are you waiting on God's timing for anything in your life?

3. "We are broken when God strips us of our self-sufficiency. Our confidence is no longer in ourselves. Any confidence we have is based on what we know God can do in us and through us." Have you ever experienced a process of being broken of your self-sufficiency so that you could rely on God?

Chapter 13: Worship

1. Dr. Evans writes, "Worship lifts you from earth into heaven." What does that statement mean to you? Can you describe a time you experienced something like that?

2. "To worship God simply means to maintain a posture or mindset in which you intentionally and actively ascribe worth to God." What practical steps can you take to incorporate that posture or mindset in your daily routine?

3. "You will know your destiny when you are living a lifestyle of worship, the lightbulb comes on, and you say, 'I've got it! That's what I've been created to do!'" Has the lightbulb ever come on for you? If so, describe that experience.

Chapter 14: Glory

1. "We see God's glory when He shows up and reveals Himself in a way that evokes a response of praise." What kinds of experiences might this include?

2. "You were created to reflect Him and His glory to a world in desperate need of seeing, experiencing, and feeling Him

and His glory." Do you know someone who effectively reflects God's glory? How might you reflect God's glory?

3. "Rather than giving God's glory a nod or a song or a two-hour block of time on a Sunday, bask in God's all-consuming presence now." What are some ways you can do that?

Chapter 15: Future

1. "People lose hope when they can't see a future." God has a future for you. What elements of your future can you focus on today that will bring you hope right now?

2. "One of the key components of a life of destiny is trust in the Lord in times that don't make sense." Does anything in your life right now not seem to make sense? What can you say to the Lord about trusting Him in that situation?

3. "Waiting on the timing of your destiny is not the same as sitting back and doing nothing. God says to become as productive as you possibly can where you are." What steps can you take to be productive right where you are?

4. "As you help others locate and live out their destinies, you set yourself up to discover your own." Whom can you help locate and live out his or her destiny?

NOTES

Chapter 1: Concept

1. Harold W. Hoehner, "Ephesians," *The Bible Knowledge Commentary: An Exposition of the Scriptures by Dallas Seminary Faculty [New Testament Edition]*, eds. John F. Walvoord and Roy B. Zuck (Wheaton, IL: Victor, 1983), 624.

Chapter 4: Completeness

2. "'Father of Aerobics' Kenneth Cooper, MD, MPH to Receive Healthy Cup Award from Harvard School of Public Health," Harvard School of Public Health, 2008. www.hsph.harvard.edu/news/press-releases/2008-releases/aerobics-kenneth-cooper-to-receive-harvard-healthy-cup-award.html.

Chapter 11: Commitment

3. See at http://www.yogiberra.com/about.html.

SCRIPTURE INDEX

ABOUT THE URBAN ALTERNATIVE

The Urban Alternative (TUA) equips, empowers, and unites Christians to impact individuals, families, churches, and communities to restore hope and transform lives.

We believe the core cause of the problems we face in our personal lives, homes, and societies is a spiritual one; therefore, the only way to address them is spiritually. We've tried political, social, economic, and even religious agendas. It's time for a kingdom agenda—God's visible and comprehensive rule over every area of life—because when we function as we were designed, God's divine power changes everything. It renews and restores as the life of Christ is made manifest within our own. As we align ourselves under Him, He brings about full restoration from deep within. This atmosphere revives and makes whole.

As it impacts us, it impacts others, transforming every sphere of life. When each biblical sphere of life functions in accordance with God's Word, the outcomes are evangelism, discipleship, and community impact. As we learn how to govern ourselves under God, we transform the institutions of family, church, and society according to a biblically based kingdom perspective. Through Him, we touch heaven and change earth.

To achieve our goal we use a variety of strategies, methods, and resources for reaching and equipping as many people as possible.

Broadcast Media

Hundreds of thousands of individuals experience *The Alternative with Dr. Tony Evans* through the daily radio broadcast on more than 500 radio outlets and in more than 40 countries. The broadcast can also be seen on several television networks and at TonyEvans.org.

Leadership Training

Kingdom Agenda Pastors (KAP) provides a viable network for like-minded pastors who embrace the kingdom agenda philosophy. Pastors have the opportunity to go deeper with Dr. Tony Evans as they are given greater biblical knowledge, practical applications, and resources to impact individuals, families, churches, and communities. KAP welcomes senior and associate pastors of all churches.

Kingdom Agenda Pastors' Summit progressively develops church leaders to meet the demands of the twenty-first century while maintaining the gospel message and the strategic position of the church. The summit includes intensive seminars, workshops, and resources, addressing issues affecting the community, family, leadership, organizational health, and more.

Pastors' Wives Ministry, founded by Dr. Lois Evans, provides counsel, encouragement, and spiritual resources for pastors' wives as they serve with their husbands in the ministry. The ministry focuses on the KAP Summit, which offers senior pastors' wives a safe place to reflect, renew, and relax along with training in personal development, spiritual growth, and care for their emotional and physical well-being. For more information, visit LoisEvans.org.

Community Impact

National Church Adopt-A-School Initiative (NCAASI) prepares churches across the country to impact communities by using public schools as the primary vehicle for effecting positive social change in urban youth and families. Leaders of churches, school districts, faith-based organizations, and other nonprofit organizations are equipped with the knowledge and tools to forge partnerships and build strong social-service delivery systems. This training is based on the comprehensive church-based community impact strategy conducted by Oak Cliff Bible Fellowship. It addresses such areas as economic development, education, housing, health revitalization, family renewal, and racial reconciliation. We also assist churches in tailoring the model to meet the specific needs of their communities while simultaneously addressing the spiritual and moral frame of reference.

Resource Development

We are fostering lifelong learning partnerships with the people we serve by providing a variety of published materials. We offer booklets, Bible studies, books, CDs, and DVDs to strengthen people in their walk with God and ministry to others.

For more information, a catalog of Dr. Tony Evans's ministry resources, and a complimentary copy of Dr. Evans's devotional newsletter,

call
(800) 800-3222

or write
The Urban Alternative
PO Box 4000, Dallas TX 75208

or log on to
TonyEvans.org

Other Harvest House Books

by Tony Evans

30 Days to Overcoming Emotional Strongholds

Emotional strongholds come in all shapes and sizes—doubt, rejection, poor self-esteem, pride, stubbornness, a victim mentality, or defeatism. Which of these are you battling? Tearing down emotional strongholds so they no longer dominate your thoughts and actions can come only through an intentional alignment of your thoughts with God's truth in the Bible. Join Dr. Tony Evans in examining key emotional strongholds and their corresponding biblical truths that you can declare and apply to bring victory into your life.

30 Days to Overcoming Addictive Behavior

Do you feel ambushed by your obsessions? Addictions come in all forms: overindulging, overspending, overworking, and more. But no matter how they show up in your life, they trap you and edge out the freedom you can enjoy in Christ. Take this 30-day journey filled with powerful biblical insights and practical tips for overcoming the behavior that controls you. You'll discover the tools and principles you need to embrace healing and find liberation.

30 Days to Victory Through Forgiveness

It happened so long ago…and yet here you are, still harboring unforgiveness for that devastating offense. Maybe it was a loved one who betrayed you, or someone you barely knew. Perhaps it's even God you're still blaming for your bitterness. The good news is that you no longer need to hold on to that festering wound. In just 30 days, you can be free from that heavy weight of offense. Allow Dr. Evans to gently lead you through the specific steps for victory over unforgiveness.

Praying Through the Names of God

Through the names of God, you gain insight into God's character—and how each name represents a facet of His being that He wants you to know and trust. In this resource, Dr. Evans reveals fascinating insights into some of God's powerful names and offers you the opportunity to benefit personally by providing prayers based on those names. Your prayer life will be revitalized as you connect your requests with the specific characteristic of God's name relevant to your need.

Horizontal Jesus

Do you want to sense God's encouragement, comfort, and love for you every day? As you give these things away to others, you'll personally experience them with God in a new way. Jesus empowers His church to be His hands and feet in the world today—to share His life in your horizontal relationships.

Discover how you can become a horizontal Jesus—a channel of God's blessings to everyone around you—using several "one another" passages of Scripture, including love one another, welcome one another, encourage one another, forgive one another, accept one another, and restore one another. As you fulfill your God-given destiny to be a conduit of God's grace, you will experience His flow of life in and through you like never before.

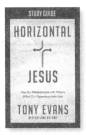

Horizontal Jesus Study Guide

This useful study guide will help you live out the horizontal Jesus message, with a chapter-by-chapter review of the book with scripture passages, questions to answer, and suggestions for practical application. Perfect for group or individual study.

Victory in Spiritual Warfare

This book unveils a simple yet radical truth: Every struggle faced in the physical realm has its root in the spiritual realm. With passion and clarity, Dr.Evans demystifies spiritual warfare so that you can tackle challenges with spiritual power—God's authority—as you understand how the battle is fought by Satan. Experience victory over your battles and embrace the life, hope, and purpose God has for you!

Prayers for Victory in Spiritual Warfare

Spiritual victory is a privilege to be enjoyed by every Christian. Why then do you seem to encounter so many obstacles in your daily life? Perhaps you have not yet learned how to stand strong in the victory that is already yours in Christ. Did you know that God has given you powerful weapons to help you withstand the onslaught of Satan's lies?

Based on Dr. Evans's life-changing book *Victory in Spiritual Warfare*, the prayers in this book will help you stand against the enemy's attacks and experience victory in all the vital areas of your life.

Watch Your Mouth

Your greatest weapon—for good or evil—is in your mouth. In this compelling resource you'll learn about taming your tongue. Discern what should or shouldn't be said so that you honor God with your speech, and develop the ability to praise God and voice wisdom even in tough circumstances. Get inspired by Tony's teaching on the tongue and let your words minister to and speak life into the world around you.

Watch Your Mouth Growth and Study Guide

Great for group or individual study, this companion guide to *Watch Your Mouth* will help you take to heart the Bible's life-changing truths about your words. Get everything you need to prompt further growth and discussion, and discover what it really means to glorify God with your mouth.

Watch Your Mouth DVD

Your words can call down destruction—or they can speak life into the world around you. Discover how to glorify God with your speech in this DVD presentation that includes four sessions of powerful teaching and moving personal testimonies.

Watch Your Mouth Interactive Workbook

Dig deep into the Bible's life-changing truths about the tongue in this companion workbook to the *Watch Your Mouth* DVD series from Dr. Tony Evans. You'll discover how to be victorious with your voice, honor God with your mouth, and avoid wrecking relationships with your words.

A Kid's Guide to the Armor of God

Tony Evans challenges tweens (ages 8 to 12) to explore what the armor of God is all about. He understands that Christian kids want to be stronger, more confident, and skilled at living an exciting God-centered life, and so he presents the unvarnished truth. When every piece of God's armor is worn correctly, the enemy is defeated and Christians finish victorious. By learning how to dress in the armor God provides, preteens are able to speak the truth, stand firm in the faith, and spread the good news of Jesus Christ.

To learn more about Harvest House books and
to read sample chapters, visit our website:

www.harvesthousepublishers.com

HARVEST HOUSE PUBLISHERS
EUGENE, OREGON